Gino's islands in the sun

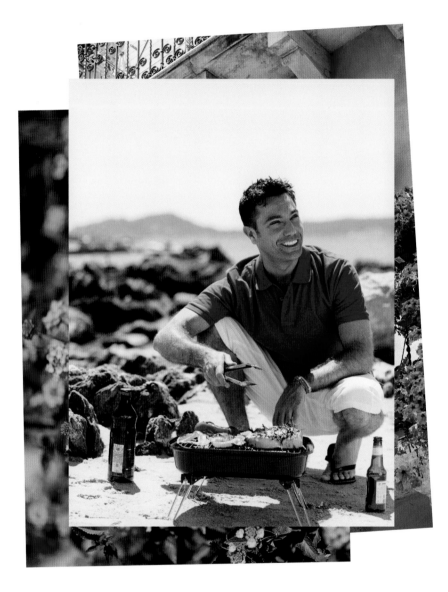

GINO'S ISLANDS IN THE SUN

OVER 100 RECIPES FROM SARDINIA & SICILY TO ENJOY AT HOME

GINO D'ACAMPO

Sardinia

Sicily

This book is dedicated to everyone who works with me – in my restaurants and other food-related businesses. A big thank you for all the support you've given me over the past 13 years – without you it would have been impossible.

INTRODUCTION

When I returned from my travels around Sardinia and Sicily, where we'd been filming *Islands in the Sun*, I was so inspired by all the diverse and wonderful dishes I'd tasted I couldn't wait to put this recipe collection together. It was fascinating comparing and contrasting the two islands – particularly as an Italian – and while they do share some common characteristics with the mainland and each another, both Sardinia and Sicily have their own extremely strong identities and distinct culinary traditions.

My journey began in Sardinia. I'm very fortunate in having a villa near Olbia, in the northeast of the island, and I thought it would be great to start the series right there – in my home. We organised a *festa* for that first night and invited a large group of my local friends. I cooked the Sardinian speciality porcheddu (spit-roasted suckling pig) and the guests brought antipasti, traditional bread soup and copious bottles of the local mirto liqueur. They were more than happy to suggest all sorts of places that I should visit; even though I spend a lot of time on the island, there was still so much I hadn't seen and had yet to discover.

Exploring Sardinia

We set off for the northwest of the island along winding mountain roads, passing prehistoric stone carvings and amazing natural rock formations. Alghero – a beautiful medieval town that looks across the sea to the northeastern coast of Spain – was our first destination. Sometimes known as Barceloneta ('Little Barcelona'), the town is famous for its strong links with Spanish and Catalan culture, evident in the architecture, local dialect and – most interesting for me - the food. I tried a number of popular local dishes, including sea-urchin linguine and menjar blanc (a Spanish-style blancmange), but one of my favourite dishes of the region was undoubtedly Catalan-style lobster, which I have included in this book.

After exploring the ancient stalactite caves at the Grotta Di Nettuno (Neptune's Grotto), we travelled into the mountains, which according to locals is where you will find the true heart of Sardinia. In times past, it was unsafe to live on the coast because of the ever-present threat of invasion, so the population retreated into the island's interior, where they farmed and raised livestock – a way of life that continues to this day. It was in the mountains where I sampled the local specialities of pecorino cheese, cold meats, ricotta with honey and pane carasau (flatbread) – all washed down with the heavenly heavy-bodied red Cannonau wine and Filu e Ferru, the local grappa. But perhaps a highlight of the day for me was cooking the traditional Sardinian pasta dish gnocchetti sardi alla campidanese (sometimes known as malloreddus alla campidanese), which consists of home-made pasta shells served with a chunky sauce made from highly seasoned sausage meat. It is simple, rustic and full of strong, punchy flavours.

While the mountains were stunning, after months of being land-locked in London I was itching to get back to the sea, so we headed to the glorious beaches of the south coast. I was able to experience the art of Sardinian fishing and also got to visit the incredible archaeological site of Nora and snorkel in the bay. It was a day I'll never forget and I cooked right there, on the beach – probably the most beautiful location in which I've ever cooked. On the menu was fresh fish, of course – tuna, straight from the sea.

Then we were off to Cagliari, the island's capital in the south of the island, from where we were to travel to Sicily. Although I love Sardinia and am always sad to leave, I couldn't wait to visit Sicily – believe it or not, I'd never visited the island so it was an entirely new adventure for me and I was really excited.

Discovering Sicily

After an overnight ferry journey we arrived in a very hot Sicily – first impressions were it was definitely busier and considerably louder than Sardinia! Palermo, the island's capital, is famous for its street food, which we simply couldn't wait to try, so that was top of our 'to do' list. There was a place in the city that I'd heard about (La Vucciria market) where many of the establishments are illegal – meaning they don't have a proper food licence – and once we arrived in the town I organised a visit with the film crew. The piazza where it all happens was very charming – loud and bustling – and the food was excellent. You can find anything from grilled octopus to coconut slices dipped in chocolate sauce, so for a passionate foodie like me it was heaven. But then all hell broke loose ... as we were filming, the local police raided the place and I found myself in the middle of the piazza with all the shops closed and people running and screaming all over the place. It was scary, I must admit, but also rather exciting to witness at first hand the lawlessness for which the island is so well known.

After exploring the extraordinary catacombs in Monreale, where the skeletons of Palermitano dignitaries from centuries ago have been preserved – some still dressed in their original clothes – we headed to Marsala, where they make the famous Italian sweet wine. I'd been looking forward to trying it and visited a vineyard where I cooked a fantastic chicken dish using Marsala, oranges and raisins. You really should try this recipe – although I say so myself, it's absolutely delicious!

Another 'must-visit' for me was a citrus farm, as oranges and lemons are among Sicily's largest exports and the islanders use them in so many dishes as well as in jams and the local limoncello liqueur. There I cooked a creamy lemon risotto using lemons plucked straight from the tree. Using such fresh lemons was a real thrill, but I've made the same risotto back home in England and can assure you it tastes wonderful here too.

While all the food in Sicily is amazing, desserts are a particular speciality and we did not hold back – magnificent ice cream, artisan chocolate and traditional desserts such as cannoli and cassata – we tried them all. I was privileged to meet master pastry chefs and chocolatiers who were so passionate and knowledgeable about their craft, using traditional methods that have been passed down through the generations to create unsurpassed culinary masterpieces.

No visit to Sicily is complete without a walk around the crater at Mount Etna – the largest active volcano in Europe. It is tremendously majestic, the view from the top is incredible and finally the crew and I could enjoy a bit of fresh air – it can get really stifling when you're doing a lot of filming under hot lights! And I personally couldn't possibly leave Sicily without fulfilling a lifelong dream – to visit the town of Savoca, where my absolute favourite movie of all time – *The Godfather* – was filmed. What can I tell you? It was *magical*. To be able to sit in Bar Vitelli on the same chair that Al Pacino used when he was filming and in the same spot where the director, Francis Ford Coppola, is said to have consumed 16 granitas daily … for me it was a dream come true.

I thoroughly enjoyed my trip around Sardinia and Sicily – they are both extremely beautiful, the people are very welcoming and passionate about their food, and the ingredients are second to none. I hope to have whetted your appetite to try some of the wonderful recipes that we discovered on our journey and which capture the flavours of the islands. I have chosen the ones that stood out most for me and, as always with my recipes, they are easy to create at home. I hope very much that you enjoy them as much as I do.

Buon appetito and Ciao!

Gino xxx

SARDINIA

Sassari

Alghero

SEA OF SARDINIA

Oristano

Isola di San Pietro

ABOUT SARDINIA

With the French island of Corsica as its closest neighbour and lying closer to North Africa than the Italian coast, Sardinia really has a very different feel from both mainland Italy and Sicily. In fact, it has been described as being to Italy what Hawaii is to the United States. Like Sicily, the landscape is mountainous and hilly, but Sardinia is much greener, more rural with wilder countryside and generally quieter. Today, the stunning coastlines attract huge numbers of tourists – particularly the Costa Smeralda, Alghero and the island's capital city Cagliari. However, the heart still belongs to the native Sardinians, who hold on to their ancient customs, traditional cuisine and unique language (Sardo) – a form of classical Latin that is spoken by over 1 million people and very distinct from modern Italian. I spend half my time in Sardinia and I never stop marvelling at the islanders' remarkable individuality and strong cultural identity.

Sardinia is in the 'Blue Zone', which means its inhabitants are among the longest-lived people in the world – a fact that is attributed in large part to their diet, which includes plenty of home-grown vegetables and fruit, pulses, wholegrain breads, pecorino cheese (which is high in omega-3 fatty acids) and meat. Fresh fish has become part of the diet relatively recently – a surprising fact given that Sardinia is completely surrounded by water. I've been told that the reason for this is because Sardinia's coast has been invaded so many times throughout its history – by the Phoenicians, Romans, Vandals, Goths, Byzantines, Arabs and Spanish – that the inhabitants found refuge in the mountains, sourcing their food and developing their dishes from the land rather than the sea. Today there are still more shepherds than fishermen in Sardinia and the shepherds lead a traditional life that has changed little for hundreds of years – they take great pride in their work and walk many miles each day – another reason perhaps for their longevity.

Sardinian cuisine varies from region to region and reflects the island's chequered history. You will notice strong Spanish, Catalan, French and Arabic influences in the food, as well as Italian, all coming together to form a dazzling array of regional styles and dishes. It was the Spanish who exerted a major influence on the wines of Sardinia, with the full-bodied red Cannonau and the white Vermentino di Gallura being the most popular today. Mirto – the liqueur made from red myrtle – is the most common *digestivo* and is sometimes used in cooking.

If you have the opportunity to travel to Sardinia, you can sample how the 'real' Sardinians make their meals by visiting an agriturismo. Basically, they are homely restaurants and farm-stays – and I do mean homely, as they can literally be in somebody's home (I well remember, on one occasion, the shock of finding toothbrushes by the sink!). You'll discover the best ones through word of mouth and they are often tucked away in very bizarre places; I've eaten in one that was located at the back of a graveyard and another that was practically hanging over a mountain edge – and they were both wonderful. Generally there is no menu; you are served six or seven dishes and the food just keeps coming – produce that your hosts have grown in their gardens, cheeses and salami made from scratch, home-made wine and meat reared on their land, usually goat, lamb or pork. The agriturismo truly is an incredible experience with an authenticity that's hard to find in many tourist restaurants.

Finally, I'd like to share these 'Sardinian Lessons for Life' with you. These are taught to children as rules to live by and although most are familiar to me, as mainland Italy has a similar ethos, I think they're well worth setting down here as a reminder of the important things in life:

1. Put family first – If you have strong family values and each person feels cared for, things aren't so hard during the bad times.

2. Celebrate your elders – Grandparents not only provide love, childcare and financial help, but carry a wealth of wisdom.

3. Laugh with friends – Visit any village in Sardinia and I guarantee you will see people sitting in their doorways chatting and enjoying life.

4. Take a walk – You will keep fit without putting stress on your joints.

5. Drink a glass of red wine daily – Red wine is considered good for the heart and Cannonau contains more antioxidants than any other wine in the world.

6. Drink goat's milk – One glass a day is thought to protect against inflammatory diseases associated with ageing, such as heart disease or Alzheimer's.

7. Always use fresh ingredients wherever possible – No GM food or preservatives for the locals!

8. Whatever the weather, go out and enjoy It whenever you can – Fresh air is vital for health and well being.

These rules may seem simple, but given the remarkably long lifespan of the Sardinians they seem to work!

ANTIPASTI & SOUPS

Sardinia

ANTIPASTI & SOUPS

Traditionally, Sardinian meals usually start with soup or a salad rather than the wide range of antipasti options we've come to expect on Italian menus. However, mainland Italy can certainly claim to have had a major influence in this area; today you'll find a mouth-watering selection of fresh meats, salamis, olives, cheese and bread wherever you go in Sardinia.

A common hot antipasti option, often served sliced, is salsiccia sarda – a type of sausage usually made from air-dried wild boar seasoned with fennel. Prosciutto crudo (cured ham) features too and seems to be more popular than bresaola and other cured meats. You will certainly always find cheese as part of a sharing platter, and Sardinia is a major exporter of both caciocavallo and pecorino cheeses – make sure you try pecorino sardo, the famous local sheep's cheese: it's one of my absolute favourites. The best way to appreciate Sardinian cheeses is with a glass of deep-red Cannonau (the local wine) and pane carasau (wafer-thin flatbread) or tarallini sardi (crisp baked dough rings).

Home-grown fresh vegetables are also widespread as antipasti - roasted, grilled, marinated in oil and vinegar and deep-fried. Naturally, along the coast you'll find a lot of seafood antipasti, including carpaccio di pesce (raw fish) and octopus salad.

The soups are fabulous in Sardinia, but if ordering one as a first course be aware that they are usually very hearty and filling as they tend to contain pulses such as lentils or chickpeas.

I have selected just a few of my favourite Sardinian antipasti here, all of which are easy to make at home. In addition, you'll find many recipes elsewhere in the book that you can serve as antipasti, for instance all the side dishes and several main courses, including the ever-popular grilled sardines ... just adjust portion sizes and quantities to suit. *Buon appetito*!

NO-COOK FENNEL & ASPARAGUS SALAD WITH PECORINO & THYME

Insalata di finocchi e asparagi crudi con pecorino e timo

This is a wonderfully simple and elegant antipasti salad for spring, with the crisp raw fennel and fresh seasonal asparagus providing an exciting contrast of textures and flavours. For a main-course salad, add some hard-boiled quails' eggs and smoked salmon. Serve with a few slices of toasted ciabatta bread.

Serves 4

2 large fennel bulbs, cored
200g fine asparagus spears, woody ends removed
150g pecorino sardo cheese

For the dressing
Juice of 1 lemon
1 teaspoon chopped fresh thyme
6 tablespoons extra virgin olive oil
Salt and freshly ground black pepper

1. Slice the fennel very finely on a mandolin or using a sharp knife. Cut off the tips of the asparagus and slice the stems into matchsticks. Place the vegetables in a large bowl.

2. To make the dressing, put the lemon juice and thyme in a small bowl. Gradually add the oil, whisking vigorously as you go, and season with salt and pepper. Pour the dressing over the vegetables and toss together to mix.

3. Cover the salad and leave to marinate at room temperature for 30 minutes, turning occasionally. Meanwhile, make shavings of pecorino using a vegetable peeler.

4. Arrange the salad on a large serving platter and scatter the pecorino over the top.

ROASTED VEGETABLES WITH HONEY, FRESH MINT & GARLIC

Verdure al forno alla Stazzu Li Paladini

Whenever I'm in Sardinia I regularly pay a visit to my friends Alessandro and Erica, who own a restaurant in Olbia called Agriturismo Stazzu Li Paladini. They serve very traditional Sardinian food and haven't got a menu – whatever they prepare on the day they serve to their customers. This dish is one of their favourites and I absolutely love it. If you prefer, you can grill the vegetables instead of roasting them, but the most important thing is to use good-quality vegetables. Serve with warm, crusty bread.

Serves 4–6

2 large red onions, peeled and cut into 12 wedges
1 large aubergine, cut into 1cm cubes
2 yellow peppers, deseeded and cut into 1cm cubes
2 large courgettes, cut into 1cm cubes
1 teaspoon dried chilli flakes
1 tablespoon chopped fresh rosemary
10 tablespoons extra virgin olive oil

1 head of broccoli, divided into bite-sized florets
150ml dry white wine
5 garlic cloves, peeled and halved
3 tablespoons runny honey
10 fresh mint leaves
Salt

1. Preheat the oven to 200°C/gas mark 6. Put the onions, aubergine, peppers and courgettes in a large, shallow roasting tin, sprinkle over the chilli flakes and rosemary and season with salt. Drizzle over the oil and, using your hands, toss all the vegetables together until well coated in the oil.

2. Roast the vegetables for 15 minutes, then add the broccoli. Mix to combine with the other vegetables and to coat the florets in oil. Roast for 10 minutes, then pour over the wine. Return to the oven to cook for a further 10–15 minutes or until tender.

3. Transfer the roasted vegetables to a dish and stir in the garlic, honey and mint. Leave to cool completely, then cover with cling film and place in the fridge for at least 5 hours.

4. Take the vegetables out of the fridge about 1 hour before serving to bring them to room temperature.

SCALLOP CARPACCIO WITH SARDINIAN FLATBREAD

Carpaccio di capesante con pane carasau

Raw seafood is a great speciality in Sardinia – the fishermen land their catch in the early morning and within hours it's on the plate and transformed with very little effort into something really delicious. Here I decided to use scallops as they are such a treat and when served raw have a particularly delicate flavour and texture – they simply melt in your mouth. Fresh scallops are available year round in the British Isles. Make sure they are super-fresh and ideally diver-caught.

Serves 4

12 large (king) scallops, trimmed
4 tablespoons extra virgin olive oil, plus extra for drizzling
Juice of 1 lemon
1 baby fennel bulb, trimmed and finely sliced
1 celery heart, finely sliced

20g bottarga (salted, dried fish roe), thinly sliced or shaved
6 discs of Sardinian flatbread (pane carasau), shop-
  bought or home-made (see page 108)
Salt and freshly ground black pepper

1. Preheat the oven to 190°C/gas mark 5. Using a very sharp knife, slice the scallops horizontally into thirds. Arrange in a single layer on 4 serving plates and cover with cling film. Use the bottom of a heavy glass to gently flatten the scallops as thinly as possible (about 2mm).

2. Remove the cling film and drizzle the scallops generously with the oil and lemon juice.

3. Scatter the fennel and celery over the scallops, season with salt and pepper and top with the bottarga. Drizzle over a little more oil.

4. Drizzle the flatbread (pane carasau) with oil and sprinkle with a little salt. Wrap in foil and bake for 6 minutes. Serve warm with the scallops.

COURGETTE FRITTERS WITH PECORINO

Frittelle di zucchine con pecorino

Whenever we are in Olbia, a port town on the northeast coast of Sardinia near my home, we order courgette fritters instead of chips. They make a great side dish or snack, but if you include cheese, as I have done here, they make a more substantial first course. Pecorino sardo, a traditional Sardinian hard cheese made from sheep's milk – is similar to the better-known pecorino romano (which despite its name is produced mainly in Sardinia) but is slightly richer and less salty. You could use either for this recipe, or Parmesan if you prefer. Serve the fritters with a green salad.

Serves 4

3 medium courgettes
1½ teaspoons salt, plus extra for seasoning
140g plain flour
1 medium egg, lightly beaten
60ml chilled sparkling water

70g freshly grated pecorino sardo cheese
½ teaspoon hot smoked paprika
1 tablespoon shredded fresh mint leaves
2 teaspoons dried oregano
About 1 litre vegetable oil for deep-frying

1. Use a vegetable peeler to peel thin strips from the courgettes, then slice them into matchsticks. Place in a colander set over the sink and sprinkle over 1 teaspoon of the salt. Leave for 1 hour to allow water to drain from the courgettes. Rinse the salt off the courgettes and squeeze out any excess moisture with your hands.

2. Place the flour in a large bowl. Make a well in the centre and add the egg. Gradually pour in the sparkling water, a little at a time, whisking until the flour is completely blended and the mixture is smooth. Stir in the pecorino, paprika, mint, oregano and remaining salt. Gently fold the courgettes into the mixture.

3. Heat a deep-fat fryer to 170°C, or heat the oil in a deep pan or a wok until very hot. To test the temperature, add a tiny piece of courgette; it will sizzle when the oil is hot enough for frying.

4. Spoon the mixture into the hot oil, 1 tablespoon at a time and so the pieces are not touching. Fry in batches without moving for 4 minutes, then turn and fry for a further 3 minutes or until golden and crispy all over. The batter should make 12 fritters.

5. Remove with a slotted spoon and drain on kitchen paper. Season with salt to taste.

WARM BEEF SALAD WITH ARTICHOKES, CHILLI & WALNUTS

Insalata calda di manzo con carciofi, peperoncino e noci

Sardinia is famous for its beef, particularly that of the *bue rosso* (red cow), which grazes the pastures of the volcanic Montiferru area in central-western Sardinia and is considered by many to provide the finest beef in Italy. For this recipe I have taken the theme of a traditional Sardinian beef salad and have added artichokes and walnuts – which really complement the juicy slices of warm beef fillet – plus fresh chilli to provide a little extra kick. Serve with Sardinian flatbread (pane carasau, see page 108).

Serves 4

400g fillet of beef (room temperature)
8 tablespoons extra virgin olive oil
280g chargrilled artichoke hearts in oil, drained
 and quartered
1 fresh, medium-hot red chilli, deseeded and finely chopped

4 tablespoons balsamic glaze
100g crispy mixed salad leaves
80g walnut halves, roughly chopped
Salt

1. Preheat a large frying pan over a medium heat. Rub the beef all over with half the oil and season with salt.

2. When the pan is very hot, lay the beef in the pan and brown on all sides including the ends. Remove the beef from the pan and leave to rest on a board. Cover with foil to keep warm.

3. Add the artichokes and chilli to the pan. Combine 60ml hot water and half the balsamic glaze and pour the mixture over the artichokes. Stir, bring to a simmer and set aside.

4. Carve the beef into slices about 5mm thick and arrange on a large serving platter. Spoon over the warm artichokes, chilli and liquid and arrange the salad leaves and walnuts on top. Drizzle over the remaining oil and balsamic glaze and sprinkle with a little salt.

CRISP BAKED DOUGH RINGS

Tarallini sardi

These crunchy little savoury biscuits make a great party food or are delicious served with cheese (particularly pecorino sardo), salamis and an aperitivo or glass of Sardinian Cannonau red wine at the start of a meal. They're hard to find in the shops but not difficult to make and it's so satisfying to make your own. You can store them for up to one week in an airtight container.

Makes about 40

1 x 7g sachet fast-action (easy blend) dried yeast
200g semolina flour
200g plain flour, plus extra for dusting

1 tablespoon fine salt
½ tablespoon freshly ground black pepper
7 tablespoons extra virgin olive oil

1. Place the yeast in a small bowl and pour over 250ml warm water. Stir to combine.

2. Place the flours in a large bowl and sprinkle over the salt and pepper. Make a well in the centre and pour in the yeast mixture and the oil. Mix together using the handle of a wooden spoon.

3. Knead the dough on a lightly floured work surface for about 5 minutes or until smooth. Shape the dough into a round and place in a large bowl. Cover with cling film and leave in a warm place for about 1 hour or until doubled in size.

4. Turn out the dough onto a lightly floured surface and knead again for about 5 minutes. Divide the dough into 4 equal-sized pieces. Using the palms of your hands, roll out each piece to make long 'ropes', each about 2cm in diameter. Cut across to make 8cm lengths.

5. Take a piece of dough and bring the ends together to make a ring shape. Press the ends together to seal. Repeat for the remaining dough rings.

6. Preheat the oven to 190°C/gas mark 5. Bring a large saucepan of water to the boil. Plunge 10 dough rings into the boiling water. After about 5 minutes, when they rise to the surface, remove with a slotted spoon and transfer to kitchen paper to dry. Repeat with the remaining dough rings.

7. Line 2 large baking sheets with baking parchment and arrange the dough rings on the lined sheet. Bake for 10 minutes. Reduce the temperature to 150°C/gas mark 2 and bake for a further 30 minutes or until golden and crispy.

STACKED SARDINIAN FLATBREAD TOPPED WITH A POACHED EGG

Pane frattau con uova in camicia

Uniquely Sardinian, pane frattau can be eaten as a first course or for breakfast, lunch or a light supper – in fact, serve this to me any time of day! It consists of layers of Sardinian flatbread (pane carasau) softened in stock and topped with tomato sauce, basil, pecorino cheese and a poached (or sometimes fried) egg. Traditionally, mutton stock would have been used but vegetable or chicken stock are more widely available these days. You can add a cheeky crispy bacon slice on top if you like.

Serves 4

1 x 700ml bottle passata (sieved tomatoes)
1 litre vegetable or chicken stock
4 large eggs
8 discs of Sardinian flatbread (pane carasau), shop-bought or home-made (see page 108)

10 fresh basil leaves, shredded
180g freshly grated pecorino sardo cheese
Extra virgin olive oil for drizzling
Salt and freshly ground black pepper

1. Heat the passata in a medium saucepan over a low heat for 10 minutes, stirring occasionally. Set aside and keep warm.

2. Heat the stock in a medium saucepan and bring to a gentle simmer. Crack an egg into a small bowl or cup and carefully slide it into the stock. Cook gently for 3 minutes over a low heat. Lift out the egg using a slotted spoon and transfer to kitchen paper to drain. Repeat for the remaining eggs. Keep warm.

3. Transfer the stock to a large, tall saucepan over a low heat. Using tongs, dip a flatbread disc (pane carasau) in the stock for about 3 seconds or until slightly softened. Alternatively, if you don't have a pan large enough to accommodate the flatbread, put the stock into a dish large enough to fit the flatbread and soak each disc for 5 seconds. Shake off excess liquid.

4. Place the flatbread on a large round serving platter and spread over 3 tablespoons of the passata. Scatter over some of the basil and 4 tablespoons of pecorino and season with pepper. Repeat the process, finishing with a flatbread.

5. Cut the stack into quarters and place a poached egg on top of each quarter. Drizzle with the oil and sprinkle with a little salt. Serve warm.

SPICY CHICKPEA & CLAM SOUP

Zuppa piccantina di ceci e vongole

Hearty soups containing pulses are very traditional in Sardinia and can be served before the meal or as a main course. In this recipe the clams are light and fresh and taste of the sea, while the chickpeas and dried chilli add depth and interest without overpowering the shellfish. For variety, fry some pancetta with the clams. Serve with warm, crusty bread and a glass of chilled Sardinian white wine.

Serves 6

1kg live clams

6 tablespoons extra virgin olive oil, plus extra for drizzling

4 garlic cloves, peeled and sliced

½ leek, finely sliced

2 teaspoons dried chilli flakes

1 tablespoon chopped fresh rosemary

2 x 400g tins of chickpeas, rinsed and drained

1 x 400g tin of chopped tomatoes

400ml hot vegetable stock

Grated zest of 1 unwaxed lemon

2 tablespoons chopped fresh flat-leaf parsley

Salt

1. Soak the clams in cold salted water for 1 hour and drain well. Scrub the shells under cold running water to remove sand and grit. Discard any open clams or clams with broken shells.

2. Heat 3 tablespoons of the oil in a large wide saucepan or frying pan with a lid over a high heat. Add the clams, cover tightly and cook, shaking the pan occasionally, for about 2 minutes or until the shells open. Strain any cooking juices from the clams and reserve.

3. When cool enough to handle, discard any clams that have not opened and remove the clam meat from the opened shells. Set the clam meat aside and discard the shells.

4. Heat the remaining oil in a medium saucepan over a medium heat. Add the garlic, leek, chilli flakes and rosemary and cook for 8 minutes, stirring occasionally.

5. Add the chickpeas, tomatoes, reserved clam juices, stock and 400ml boiling water and stir to combine. Bring to the boil over a high heat then reduce the heat and simmer gently for about 20 minutes. Skim off any scum that rises to the surface.

6. Stir in the reserved clam meat, the lemon zest and half the parsley and simmer for 10 minutes. Remove from the heat and season with salt.

7. Ladle into warm soup bowls, drizzle over a little oil and sprinkle over the remaining parsley.

PASTA, RISOTTO & PIZZA

Sardinia

PASTA, RISOTTO & PIZZA

As is usual throughout most of Italy, pasta and risotto are served as a first course in Sardinia. The ingredients should be the best you can afford and the dishes served with minimal garnishing – Sardinians like their food simply prepared so the natural flavours can best be appreciated.

All the usual pasta shapes that you would expect to find in Italy can also be found in Sardinia, but probably the most common and distinctive Sardinian pasta shape has to be gnocchetti sardi or malloreddus. Made from semolina and sometimes saffron, they have a rigid shell-like shape that is perfect for holding the sauce, which is usually made from highly seasoned pork sausage, as in the hearty dish gnocchetti sardi alla campidanese. Traditionally, most pasta is served with a rich meaty sauce in Sardinia, but lobster, clams and bottarga (the salted, dried roe of grey mullet or tuna) are common alternatives nowadays. Sardinian cooks use bottarga liberally, grating or shaving it onto pasta and pizzas.

Risotto in Sardinia is also often made with meat – in some cases three or four different kinds – and mushrooms are also quite common, as the mountains produce such a great array. One of my favourite risotto recipes from Sardinia contains pork, mixed cheeses and sage – it's hearty and rich and extremely flavoursome. Seafood and vegetable risottos are also prevalent, served before a meaty meal.

When it comes to pizza, I admit to being rather biased, as for me the best pizza in the world comes from southern Italy. However, I was surprised to learn that archaeologists in Sardinia have discovered evidence of a flatbread very similar to pizza dating back 7,000 years – so maybe it originated there all along! All the familiar varieties of topping are found on the island, but pecorino sardo (the local sheep's cheese) often replaces the more familiar mozzarella or Parmesan.

For this chapter I've selected a range of recipes for vegetarians, fish-eaters and carnivores and have included quick-cook and prepare-ahead recipes for all occasions. I'm sure there will be something for everyone.

SPAGHETTINI WITH MUSSELS, CHERRY TOMATOES & WHITE WINE

Spaghettini alle cozze, pomodorini e vino bianco

I love recipes that require just a few good-quality ingredients and are simple to make yet really have the 'wow factor', such as this pasta dish with mussels. You don't have to use the bottarga – the dish stands alone without it – but a Sardinian cook would almost certainly grate it over the top of the finished dish.

Serves 4

800g live mussels
150ml dry white wine
6 tablespoons extra virgin olive oil
2 garlic cloves, peeled and sliced
15 fresh red cherry tomatoes, halved
4 tablespoons chopped fresh flat-leaf parsley

500g dried spaghettini
60g bottarga (salted, dried fish roe), freshly grated
 (optional)
Salt and freshly ground black pepper

1. Scrub the mussels under cold running water. Rinse away grit and remove barnacles with a small, sharp knife. Remove the 'beards' by pulling the dark, stringy piece away from the mussel. Discard any open mussels or mussels with broken shells.

2. Place the mussels in a large saucepan and pour over the wine. Cover and cook over a high heat for about 5 minutes or until the mussels open, shaking the pan occasionally. Tip into a colander placed over a bowl. Reserve the cooking liquid. Discard any mussels that remain closed.

3. In the same pan, heat the oil over a medium heat. Add the garlic and fry until it begins to sizzle. Add the tomatoes and parsley and pour in the reserved cooking liquid. Simmer gently for about 2 minutes. Season with salt and pepper.

4. Meanwhile, cook the spaghettini in a large pan of boiling, salted water until al dente. Drain the pasta thoroughly and tip it into the saucepan with the sauce. Add half the mussels and gently stir to combine over a low heat for 30 seconds.

5. To serve, put the pasta in large bowls, arrange the remaining mussels on top and sprinkle with the grated bottarga (if using).

HOME-MADE SARDINIAN PASTA SHELLS

Gnocchetti sardi fatti in casa

Making pasta can be a bit of a chore, but gnocchetti sardi (also known as malloreddus) is really easy. You don't need a pasta machine – just mix, roll, shape and cook. Unlike most other types of home-made pasta, which contain eggs, the dough for these shells is made from flour and water, giving the pasta a firmer texture. The shells are best served with a chunky sauce such as a ragù made from spicy Italian pork sausages (see page 42) or clams (see page 44). You can prepare the shells a day before you need them, but store them in a cool, dry place on a floured tray.

Serves 4

500g '00' grade pasta flour, plus extra for dusting
½ teaspoon fine salt

1. Place the flour in a large bowl. Make a well in the centre. Pour in 300ml warm water and sprinkle over the salt. Using the handle of a wooden spoon, gradually mix the flour into the liquid and stir well to combine. Once the texture is crumbly, like breadcrumbs, turn out the mixture onto a well-floured work surface.

2. Use your hands to bring the dough together and knead for 2 minutes. You want to create a pliable dough. If it becomes too soft, add a little more flour.

3. Divide the dough into 6 pieces and roll each piece beneath the palms of your hands to make several long 'ropes', each about the thickness of your little finger. Use a sharp knife to cut across to make 1cm pieces. Dust with a little flour.

4. Place a piece of dough on the very fine side of a grater and press against it using your thumb to flatten slightly so that the imprint makes little nodules on one side of the shells.

5. Place the prepared shells in a single layer on a floured tray until you are ready to cook them.

6. Cook the gnocchetti in a large pan of boiling, salted water for about 2 minutes or until they float to the surface. Drain thoroughly and serve with a sauce of your choice.

SARDINIAN PASTA SHELLS WITH ITALIAN SAUSAGE & TOMATO RAGÙ

Gnocchetti sardi alla campidanese

This is rustic Sardinian food at its best – simple, inexpensive ingredients but bursting with flavour. I strongly recommend you use Italian sausages for this recipe, available from Italian delicatessens and many large supermarkets – they are slightly coarser and more highly seasoned than most British sausages (sometimes including fennel, garlic and wine) – but any pure pork sausages would be fine provided you season the dish well. You can make your own pasta shells (see page 40) or look for them in Italian speciality stores or online (they may be called malloreddus). Alternatively, any other short pasta shape will do the job.

Serves 4

4 tablespoons extra virgin olive oil
1 celery stick, finely chopped
1 onion, peeled and finely chopped
1 carrot, peeled and finely chopped
1 tablespoon chopped fresh rosemary
400g coarse, Italian-style pork sausages, skin removed

2 tablespoons tomato purée
2 x 400g tins of chopped tomatoes
500g home-made Sardinian pasta shells (see page 40)
10 fresh basil leaves, shredded
80g freshly grated pecorino sardo cheese
Salt and freshly ground black pepper

1. Heat the oil in a large frying pan over a medium heat. Add the celery, fry for 1 minute, then add the onion, carrot and rosemary and season with salt. Fry for 7–8 minutes, stirring occasionally.

2. Add the sausage meat, break it up with a wooden spoon and fry for 5–8 minutes or until browned.

3. Add the tomato purée and tomatoes and simmer for about 5 minutes. Pour in 250ml water, bring to the boil then reduce the heat and simmer gently for 20 minutes, stirring occasionally. Season with salt and pepper.

4. Cook the pasta shells in a large pan of boiling, salted water for about 2 minutes or until they float to the surface. Drain thoroughly.

5. Tip the pasta shells into the sauce, add the basil and stir for 30 seconds to combine. Sprinkle over the pecorino and mix once again. Serve immediately.

SARDINIAN PASTA SHELLS WITH CLAMS, WALNUTS, CHILLI & BOTTARGA

Gnocchetti sardi con vongole, noci, peperoncino e bottarga

This recipe is often served on the coast in northern Sardinia and it's one of my favourites. In fact, I've started to make this dish at home at least once a week as I love the flavours so much. Try to get hold of bottarga if you can – it really will enhance the dish – and please don't be tempted to sprinkle cheese on top, as it will fight with the flavours of the seafood.

Serves 4

1kg live clams
120ml extra virgin olive oil
3 garlic cloves, peeled and finely sliced
½ teaspoon dried chilli flakes
40ml dry white wine

60g bottarga (salted, dried fish roe), freshly grated
500g home-made Sardinian pasta shells (see page 40)
3 tablespoons chopped fresh flat-leaf parsley
50g walnut halves, roughly chopped
Salt

1. Soak the clams in cold salted water for 1 hour, drain well and scrub the shells under cold running water. Discard any open clams or clams with broken shells.

2. Heat 80ml of the oil in a large frying pan or wok over a medium heat. Add the garlic and chilli flakes and fry for 30 seconds. Tip in the clams then pour over the wine and cover. Cook for 2 minutes or until the shells open, shaking the pan occasionally.

3. Remove the pan from the heat and discard any clams that have not opened. Remove half the clams from their shells and add the clam meat to the pan; discard the empty shells. Stir in half the bottarga and cook for 1 minute over a medium heat.

4. Meanwhile, cook the pasta shells in a large pan of boiling, salted water for about 2 minutes or until they float to the top. Drain and add to the clams. Pour over the remaining oil; stir for 30 seconds. Add the parsley, walnuts and remaining bottarga. Serve immediately.

BAKED RIGATONI WITH SPICY MEATBALLS

Rigatoni al forno con polpettine piccanti

This meatball and pasta bake is the perfect supper for a busy family, as you can prepare the dish in the morning and simply pop it in the oven when you're ready to eat. In Sardinia, meatballs are usually made with minced pork rather than beef, but by all means use beef mince if you prefer. If you can't find smoked provolone, use a mixture of mozzarella and smoked Cheddar. Serve with a side salad.

Serves 6

8 tablespoons olive oil
1 large red onion, peeled and finely chopped
3 x 400g tins of chopped tomatoes
10 fresh basil leaves
250g minced pork
100g Italian salami, rind removed and finely chopped
60g fresh white breadcrumbs
½ teaspoon chilli powder

1 medium egg, beaten
4 tablespoons plain flour
300g dried rigatoni
200g smoked provolone cheese, drained and cut into
  2cm chunks
150g freshly grated pecorino sardo cheese
Salt and freshly ground black pepper

1. First make a tomato sauce. Heat 5 tablespoons of the oil in a medium saucepan over a medium heat. Add the onion and fry gently for 5 minutes, stirring occasionally. Add the tomatoes and basil and cook over a low heat for 40 minutes, stirring frequently. Season with salt and pepper and set aside.

2. Meanwhile, to prepare the meatballs place the pork in a bowl with the salami, breadcrumbs, chilli powder, egg and some salt. Mix well with your hands until well combined. Using dampened hands, take small amounts of the pork mixture and roll into 4–5cm balls. Put the flour on a large plate or tray. Lightly roll the meatballs in the flour until evenly coated.

3. Heat the remaining oil in a large frying pan over a medium heat. Add the meatballs and fry in batches for 5 minutes or until browned, turning carefully. Remove and drain on kitchen paper.

4. Preheat the oven to 190°C/gas mark 5. Cook the rigatoni in a large pan of boiling, salted water for 3 minutes less than stated on the packet (they will continue to cook in the oven). Drain well and tip them back into the same pan. Pour over the tomato sauce, add the meatballs and gently stir to combine.

5. Tip half the pasta mixture into a large baking dish measuring about 25 x 32cm and scatter over half the provolone and half the pecorino. Add the rest of the pasta mixture and top with the remaining cheeses. Bake for 25 minutes until golden brown and bubbling on top. Leave to rest for 5 minutes out of the oven, then serve.

PENNETTE WITH SALTED RICOTTA, CHERRY TOMATOES & FRESH MINT

Pennette con ricotta salata, pomodorini e menta

You'll find ricotta salata (salted ricotta) all over Sardinia, especially in the Sassari area in the northwest. It is basically ricotta that has been salted, dried and matured; the texture is hard and crumbly and the flavour is deliciously salty and sharp. If you can't find salted ricotta, use pecorino cheese for this recipe. Pennette is simply a shorter, thinner version of penne and you can easily substitute it with penne rigate.

Serves 4

8 tablespoons extra virgin olive oil
1 garlic clove, peeled and finely sliced
300g fresh red cherry tomatoes, quartered
500g dried pennette rigate

200g freshly grated ricotta salata cheese
8 fresh mint leaves, shredded
Salt and freshly ground black pepper

1. Heat the oil in a medium frying pan over a medium heat. Add the garlic and tomatoes and fry for 1 minute, stirring continuously. Season with salt and pepper and set aside.

2. Cook the pennette in a large pan of boiling, salted water until al dente. Drain the pasta thoroughly and tip it back into the same saucepan you cooked it in. Keep it off the heat.

3. Add the tomato and garlic mixture, then the ricotta and mint. Stir to combine for 30 seconds to allow all the flavours to combine. Serve immediately.

PORK & SAGE RISOTTO

Risotto con maiale e salvia

Pork is so prevalent in Sardinia that I wanted to try it in a risotto, paired with sage – its ideal partner. I was concerned the meat might dry out, but marinating the pork in red wine vinegar keeps it really moist, adds great flavour, and the vinegar's piquancy prevents the creamy risotto from being over-rich. Towards the end of the cooking time, test whether the risotto is done by biting into a grain of rice. It should be tender but still have firmness. A couple of minutes can make all the difference between the perfect texture and a stodgy mass, so make sure you stay by your pot.

Serves 4

300g pork tenderloin (pork fillet), cut into 1cm cubes
50ml red wine vinegar
6 tablespoons extra virgin olive oil
1 large red onion, peeled and finely chopped
300g Arborio or Carnaroli rice
120ml dry white wine

1.3 litres hot beef or chicken stock
60g salted butter
80g freshly grated pecorino sardo cheese
6 large sage leaves, shredded
Salt and freshly ground black pepper

1. Place the pork in a large bowl, pour over the vinegar and season with salt and pepper. Stir to combine and set aside at room temperature.

2. Heat the oil in a medium saucepan over a medium heat. Add the onion and fry for 5 minutes, stirring, until softened but not browned.

3. Meanwhile, drain the pork and pat dry with kitchen paper. Add it to the pan with the onion and fry for about 3–5 minutes or until browned on all sides. Add the rice and stir constantly for 2 minutes or until the grains are coated and shiny.

4. Pour over the wine and simmer for about 1 minute until it has evaporated. Add 2 ladlesful of stock, bring to a simmer and stir until all the stock is absorbed. Continue adding the rest of the stock in the same way, stirring and waiting for it to be absorbed before adding more, until the rice is cooked but still has a slight bite. It should take about 16–18 minutes. You may not need to add all the stock.

5. Remove the pan from the heat and add the butter, pecorino and sage, stirring for about 30 seconds until creamy. Season with some salt and pepper and serve immediately.

COURGETTE & SAFFRON RISOTTO

Risotto con zucchine e zafferano

Saffron, sometimes referred to as 'red gold' because of its deep ruby-red colour, flourishes in the fertile hills of Sardinia's Medio Campinado province, in southwestern Sardinia. The locals use it liberally in their cooking, but given its high price in Britain I tend to use it sparingly and in dishes where it will be one of the star attractions such as this delicately flavoured risotto. The courgette flowers add colour and flavour, but they are not essential.

Serves 4

½ teaspoon saffron threads

1.3 litres hot vegetable stock

6 tablespoons olive oil

1 large onion, peeled and finely chopped

400g Arborio or Carnaroli rice

150ml dry white wine

2 medium courgettes, cut into 5mm pieces

4 courgette flowers (optional), cut into quarters lengthways

100g salted butter

80g freshly grated pecorino sardo cheese

Salt and white pepper

1. Put the saffron in a small bowl, add 4 tablespoons of the stock and set aside.

2. Heat the oil in a large, heavy-based saucepan over a medium heat. Add the onion and fry gently for 5 minutes, stirring, until softened but not browned. Add the rice and stir constantly for 2 minutes or until the grains are coated and shiny.

3. Pour over the wine and simmer for about 1 minute until it has evaporated. Stir in the saffron mixture. Add 2 ladlesful of the remaining stock, bring to a simmer and stir until all the stock is absorbed. Continue adding the stock in the same way, stirring and waiting for it to be absorbed before adding more.

4. After about 6 minutes, add the courgettes and the courgette flowers (if using), then continue with the stirring and adding of the remaining stock for a further 8–10 minutes or until the rice is cooked but still has a slight bite. You may not need to use all the stock.

5. Remove the pan from the heat and add the butter and pecorino, stirring for about 30 seconds until creamy. Season with some salt and pepper and serve immediately.

PIZZA TOPPED WITH ARTICHOKES, PECORINO & MOZZARELLA

Pizza ai carciofi, pecorino e mozzarella

If you aren't keen on tomatoes, this is the perfect pizza for you. It is also a good choice for those who don't eat meat or fish, but isn't suitable for strict vegetarians because of the cheeses. Although the ingredients seem simple, they combine beautifully – it is a classic example of 'less is more'. Do try to find pecorino sardo cheese if possible, as its tangy, salty-sweet flavour will really 'lift' this pizza.

Makes 2

200g strong white flour, plus extra for dusting
1 x 7g sachet fast-action (easy blend) dried yeast
¾ teaspoon salt
2 tablespoons extra virgin olive oil, plus extra for greasing

For the topping
2 x 125g balls of mozzarella cheese, drained and sliced
8 chargrilled artichoke hearts in oil, drained and quartered
60g freshly grated pecorino sardo cheese
10 small fresh basil leaves
Extra virgin olive oil for drizzling
Salt and freshly ground black pepper

1. Place the flour in a large bowl. Add the yeast to one side of the bowl and the salt to the other. Make a well in the centre and add the oil then gradually pour in 140ml warm water and mix together using the handle of a wooden spoon.

2. Knead the dough on a lightly floured surface for about 5 minutes or until soft, smooth and elastic.

3. Shape the dough into a round and place in a large oiled bowl. Brush the top with a little oil and cover with cling film. Leave to rest at room temperature for 20 minutes. Brush 2 baking sheets with oil and set aside. Preheat the oven to 220°C/gas mark 7.

4. Turn out the dough onto a lightly floured surface and knead just 3 or 4 times to knock out the air.

5. Halve the dough and roll out each half directly onto an oiled baking sheet, rolling and stretching the dough to make 2 rounds about 25cm in diameter and 1–2cm thick. Make a small rim by pulling up the edges slightly.

6. To make the topping, scatter the mozzarella evenly over the surface of the pizza bases, avoiding the rim. Arrange the artichokes on top and sprinkle over the pecorino. Season with salt and pepper.

7. Bake for 12–14 minutes or until golden brown. Remove from the oven, scatter over the basil and return to the oven for 1 minute. Drizzle with oil and serve immediately.

PIZZA WITH A TUNA, OLIVE & BOTTARGA TOPPING

Pizza al tonno, olive e bottarga

There are olive groves all over Sardinia, particularly in the centre and north of the island. Sardinian olives tend to be smaller than other Italian olives, but their flavour packs a large punch and it is no surprise that they are loved by locals and used liberally in their cooking. I adore the combination of green olives and tuna on a pizza, and the addition of bottarga makes it extra special.

Makes 2

200g strong white flour, plus extra for dusting
1 x 7g sachet fast-action (easy blend) dried yeast
¾ teaspoon salt
2 tablespoons extra virgin olive oil, plus extra for greasing

For the topping
150g passata (sieved tomatoes)
150g tinned chopped tomatoes, drained
3 tablespoons extra virgin olive oil

1 teaspoon dried oregano
40g capers, drained and roughly chopped
3 x 160g tins of tuna chunks in oil, drained
15 pitted green olives, drained and halved
3 garlic cloves, peeled and finely sliced
50g bottarga (salted, dried fish roe), thinly sliced or shaved
Salt and freshly ground black pepper

1. Place the flour in a large bowl. Add the yeast to one side of the bowl and the salt to the other. Make a well in the centre and add the oil then gradually pour in 140ml warm water and mix together using the handle of a wooden spoon.

2. Knead the dough on a lightly floured surface for about 5 minutes or until soft, smooth and elastic.

3. Shape the dough into a round and place in a large oiled bowl. Brush the top with a little oil and cover with cling film. Leave to rest at room temperature for 20 minutes. Brush 2 baking sheets with oil and set aside. Preheat the oven to 220°C/gas mark 7.

4. Turn out the dough onto a lightly floured surface and knead just 3 or 4 times to knock out the air.

5. Halve the dough and roll out each half directly onto an oiled baking sheet, rolling and stretching the dough to make 2 rounds about 25cm in diameter and 1–2cm thick. Make a small rim by pulling up the edges slightly.

6. To make the topping, put the passata and tomatoes in a medium bowl with 1 tablespoon of the oil. Stir in the oregano and capers and season with salt and pepper. Spread the mixture evenly over the surface of the pizza bases, avoiding the rim. Arrange the tuna and olives on top and drizzle 1 tablespoon of oil over each pizza.

7. Bake for about 12 minutes or until golden brown. Remove from the oven, scatter over the garlic and return to the oven for 2 minutes. Scatter over the bottarga and serve immediately.

MAIN COURSES

Sardinia

MAIN COURSES

Sardinians love their meat, although generally it tends to be eaten in small quantities only a few times a week. One of the most famous and celebratory of all their meat dishes is porcheddu (suckling pig). It's perfect for large gatherings and is honestly the best pork I've ever eaten. I've included the recipe in this chapter, served with cinnamon-flavoured apple sauce, as I'm quite sure you'll want to give it a try. Other Sardinian specialities include wild boar and baby goat, spit-roasted or in a stew, and rabbit, often cooked in mirto (the local liqueur made from red myrtle).

There are many other meats that are commonly eaten on the island but which tend to appeal less to British visitors, who can be squeamish – horse and donkey steaks are viewed as no different from beef steaks in Sardinia, and spicy tripe stew and lamb offal skewers are common fare, particularly in the north of the island. I've included only 'mainstream' meats in this book, but if you go to Sardinia I urge you to try some of the more unusual offerings and I'm sure you'll be pleasantly surprised.

Of course, Sardinians are very skilled fishermen. They catch mainly tuna, especially from Carloforte – a fishing town on the Isola di San Pietro, 4km off the southwest coast of Sardinia. No part of the fish goes to waste: the eggs become bottarga (dried, salted roe), the fillet becomes musciame and is thinly sliced, just like ham; then there are the cuts known as ventresca and tarantella – they are less fatty and more pleasing to the palate. Grey mullet is used in similar ways, and sea bass is always popular, either cooked whole or as fillets. The lobsters from Alghero (in the west) are excellent and Costa Smeralda (in the north) offers sardines to die for. I've selected recipes for many of these in this chapter.

I've also included some vegetable-based main courses – an artichoke tart, a baked mushroom dish and a savoury bread pudding. All are delicious, traditional recipes that really capture the tastes of Sardinia.

ARTICHOKE, RED ONION & ROCKET TART

Torta di carciofi, cipolle rosse e rucola

Artichokes are so popular in Sardinia that in Sassari – the island's second largest city, located in the northwest – a festival is held in March each year to celebrate the great vegetable. This artichoke tart is basically a French-style quiche – with Corsica as Sardinia's closest neighbour there is a French influence in Sardinian cuisine – but it contains Italian rather than French cheeses. I like the peppery flavour of rocket here, but you can substitute it with spinach leaves if you prefer. Serve with a side salad.

Serves 8

4 tablespoons olive oil

2 red onions, peeled and finely sliced

8 chargrilled artichoke hearts in oil, drained and halved

Butter for greasing

Plain flour for dusting

400g shop-bought shortcrust pastry

400g rocket, roughly chopped

6 large eggs

60g freshly grated pecorino sardo cheese

100g ricotta cheese

Salt and white pepper

1. Preheat the oven to 190°C/gas mark 5. Heat the oil in a large frying pan over a medium heat. Add the onions and fry for 6 minutes or until softened, stirring occasionally. Add the artichokes, cover and cook for 4 minutes.

2. Grease a 25cm loose-bottomed flan tin (ideally fluted) with butter. On a lightly floured surface, roll out the pastry and use it to line the tin. Chill in the freezer for 10 minutes.

3. 'Blind bake' the pastry case: prick the pastry base all over with a fork, line the bottom and sides with baking parchment and weigh it down with baking beans. Place on a baking sheet and bake for 10 minutes. Remove the beans and paper, return to the oven and bake for a further 3 minutes. Set aside to cool.

4. Reduce the oven temperature to 160°C/gas mark 3. Put the rocket in a colander set over the sink and pour over boiling water to soften. Squeeze out excess water and set aside.

5. Lightly beat the eggs in a large bowl and add the cheeses, rocket and some salt and pepper. Stir to combine. Add the artichoke and onion mixture. Stir again. Turn the mixture into the cooled pastry case, spreading it out evenly.

6. Bake for 25–30 minutes or until the filling is golden and just set. Remove from the oven and allow the tart to cool in its tin for 10 minutes before serving. Serve warm.

MUSHROOM, CHEESE & SARDINIAN FLATBREAD BAKE

Sformato di pane carasau con funghi e formaggio

I first tried this recipe in a remote restaurant in the mountains of Sardinia. It is similar to lasagne, with its layers of béchamel, cheese and mushrooms, but wafer-thin Sardinian flatbread (pane carasau) is used instead of pasta sheets. The combination of earthy mushrooms with the creamy béchamel and pungent cheeses is truly a match made in heaven. Serve with a little green salad.

Serves 6

5 tablespoons olive oil

250g chestnut mushrooms, sliced

250g button mushrooms, halved

30g dried porcini mushrooms, soaked in hot water, drained
  and sliced

500ml hot vegetable stock

2 discs of Sardinian flatbread (pane carasau),
  shop-bought or home-made (see page 108)

Salted butter for greasing

180g Taleggio cheese, rind removed and cut into
  small pieces

80g freshly grated pecorino sardo cheese

Salt and freshly ground black pepper

For the béchamel

100g salted butter

100g plain flour

1 litre full-fat milk

Pinch of freshly grated nutmeg

1. Preheat the oven to 190°C/gas mark 5. Heat the oil in a large frying pan over a high heat. Add all the mushrooms, season with salt and pepper and fry for 5 minutes, stirring occasionally. Transfer to kitchen paper to drain.

2. To make the béchamel sauce, melt the butter in a medium saucepan over a medium heat until foaming. Add the flour and cook for 1–2 minutes until pale golden, stirring continuously. Now start adding the milk a little at a time, whisking constantly and waiting for it to be incorporated before adding more.

3. Bring the sauce to the boil then reduce the heat and simmer gently for 5–10 minutes, whisking occasionally, until thickened and smooth.

4. Add the nutmeg and season with salt and pepper. Remove from the heat and set aside.

5. Pour the stock into a dish large enough to fit the flatbread. Soak each disc in the stock for 5 seconds each side. Discard the stock.

6. Lay a soaked flatbread disc on the bottom of a greased round baking dish, 35cm in diameter. Spread over half the béchamel and scatter over three quarters of the mushrooms. Dot over the Taleggio and place a second piece of soaked flatbread on top. Spread over the remaining béchamel and scatter over the remaining mushrooms. Sprinkle with the pecorino and pepper. Bake for 15 minutes or until golden brown. Cut into wedges and serve hot.

SAVOURY BREAD PUDDING

Zuppa gallurese

This is the ultimate comfort food, from the mountainous region of Gallura in northern Sardinia. Despite its Italian name, this is more of a savoury bread pudding or bake than a soup – a truly luscious combination of warm, crusty bread turned soft and fluffy by being drenched in stock, lots of oozing melted cheese, fresh basil and mint and a crisp, golden cheese topping. If you can't find provolone dolce, use Cheddar or mozzarella instead. Tuck in and enjoy!

Serves 6

250g freshly grated pecorino sardo cheese
6 fresh basil leaves, shredded
8 fresh mint leaves, shredded
Olive oil for greasing
1 large, stale country-style loaf of bread (with crusts), cut
 into slices 2cm thick

1 litre hot beef or vegetable stock
8–10 large thin slices provolone dolce cheese
Salt and white pepper

1. Preheat the oven to 190°C/gas mark 5. Put the pecorino in a small bowl and stir in the basil and mint.

2. Grease a 2-litre baking dish with oil. Arrange a layer of bread in the bottom of the dish. Pour over a quarter of the stock. Prick the bread with a fork and leave for 2 minutes to soak up all the stock. Add another quarter of the stock until the bread won't absorb any more.

3. Sprinkle over half the pecorino mixture, cover with half the provolone and season with salt and pepper. Top with another layer of bread, making sure that you fill any gaps, and soak with the stock as previously; you may not need all the stock. Scatter over the remaining pecorino mixture, cover with the remaining provolone and season again.

4. Bake for 1 hour or until the bread slices on the top are golden brown and crisp. Remove from the oven and leave to rest for 10 minutes then serve.

SEMOLINA-CRUSTED FRESH TUNA MARINATED IN TOMATOES & OLIVES

Cotolette di tonno fresco e semolina con marinatura di pomodori freschi e olive

Tuna has been fished in Sardinia for thousands of years and is central to the islanders' diet. When I was filming the TV series, I cooked this fresh from the sea in southern Sardinia after visiting the amazing Roman ruins at Nora. It's a kind of posh tuna salad and the flavour and texture combinations are truly heavenly. Make sure you buy sustainable tuna, ideally approved by the MSC (Marine Stewardship Council), and use good-quality olives. Serve with lots of warm, crusty bread to mop up the sauce.

Serves 4

8 tablespoons extra virgin olive oil

4 garlic cloves, peeled and lightly crushed

500g large fresh plum tomatoes, quartered and deseeded, and each quarter cut in half lengthways

100g whole pitted green olives

350ml white wine vinegar

4 bay leaves

500g piece of fresh tuna loin

About 1 litre vegetable oil for deep-frying

80g coarse semolina

Salt and freshly ground black pepper

1. To make the marinade, heat the olive oil in a large frying pan over a low heat. Add the garlic and fry gently for 1 minute. Stir in the tomatoes and olives and season with salt and pepper. Cook for 2 minutes, stirring occasionally. Pour over the vinegar and add the bay leaves. Stir and cook for 6 minutes.

2. Cut the tuna into 2cm-thick slices across the grain. Put the semolina on a large plate or tray. Dip the tuna slices in the semolina to coat.

3. Heat a deep-fat fryer to 190°C, or heat the vegetable oil in a deep pan or a wok until very hot. To test the temperature, add a tiny piece of bread; it will sizzle when the oil is hot enough for frying.

4. Place the tuna carefully in the hot oil. Fry without moving for 1 minute, then turn and fry for a further minute or until golden all over. You may need to fry in batches. Remove with a slotted spoon and transfer to kitchen paper to drain.

5. Place the tuna in a shallow, non-metallic dish and pour over the marinade. Set aside to cool. Cover and refrigerate for 10–24 hours, turning occasionally.

6. Remove from the fridge about 1 hour before serving and discard the bay leaves. Place the tuna in a serving dish and pour over the marinade.

CHARGRILLED SARDINES WITH A CAPER & PARSLEY VINAIGRETTE

Sardine alla griglia con salsa di capperi e prezzemolo

It is widely believed that sardines were named after Sardinia, where they were among the first fish to be packed in oil. Today they are still relatively abundant in the island's coastal waters and form a major part of the islanders' diet. Pilchards are the same species but just older and larger; they can be used for this recipe too, although I prefer the flavour of young sardines. As well as tasting fantastic, this dish is also very rich in omega 3 and vitamin B. Don't worry about the bones; grilling the fish enables you to pull them out almost in one go. Try it with Fregola Salad (see page 96).

Serves 4

16 fresh sardines, scaled and gutted
200ml extra virgin olive oil
60ml red wine vinegar
Juice of 1 lemon

100g capers, drained and chopped
3 tablespoons chopped fresh flat-leaf parsley
Salt and freshly ground black pepper

1. Preheat a ridged cast-iron chargrill pan over a high heat. Rinse the sardines inside and out and pat dry with kitchen paper. Brush all over with 60ml of the oil and season with salt and pepper.

2. To make the vinaigrette, put the vinegar, lemon juice, capers and parsley in a medium bowl and whisk in the remaining oil. Season with salt and pepper and set aside.

3. When the chargrill pan is very hot, reduce the heat to medium and lay the sardines in the pan. Cook for 4 minutes or until the sardines are golden with charred grill marks, then gently turn and cook for a further 4 minutes. If you turn the fish too early, the skin will stick and tear, so don't rush it.

4. Place the sardines on a warm plate, drizzle over the vinaigrette and serve immediately.

WHOLE SEA BASS COOKED IN WHITE WINE WITH KALAMATA OLIVES

Spigola intera al forno con vino bianco e olive kalamata

Sardinians eat a lot of sea bass and serve it in many different ways. Here the whole fish is cooked in wine, which brings out its clean, delicate flavours and makes it beautifully succulent. Kalamata olives are Greek rather than Sardinian, but I just love their meaty, smooth flavour and they go so well with the fish. Sea bass is also found off the coast of Britain, but you may need to order it from your fishmonger. Try this dish with Warm Potato Salad (see page 106).

Serves 4

1 whole sea bass, about 1.5kg, scaled, gutted, gilled, fins
  and tail trimmed and head removed
500ml dry white wine (preferably Vermentino)
500ml hot fish stock
150g whole pitted Kalamata olives, drained

5 garlic cloves, peeled and finely sliced
160g salted butter, cut into small cubes
3 tablespoons chopped fresh flat-leaf parsley
Salt and freshly ground black pepper

1. Preheat the oven to 220°C/gas mark 7. Using a sharp knife, score the fish skin on one side, making 6 diagonal cuts just through to the bones. Season both sides with salt and pepper.

2. Put the wine, stock, olives and garlic in a large roasting tin over a high heat and bring to the boil. Remove from the hob, add the fish and cover tightly with foil. Cook in the oven for 25 minutes (you know the fish is cooked when the flesh near the bone at the thickest part turns white).

3. Leaving the juices in the pan, carefully transfer the whole fish to a warm serving platter and cover loosely with foil to keep warm.

4. Place the roasting tin on the hob over a high heat and boil the cooking juices until reduced by about one third, stirring occasionally. Reduce the heat, gradually stir in the butter then the parsley. Spoon the sauce over the fish and serve immediately.

CATALAN-STYLE LOBSTER

Aragosta alla catalana

Along the coast of northwestern Sardinia, which faces Spain, Catalan culture permeates the area in all sorts of ways , influencing the local dialect, the architecture, and the food. When I visited the lovely medieval city of Alghero (known as 'Little Barcelona'), I found numerous Catalan dishes on restaurant menus, particularly seafood dishes such as paella and this dressed lobster recipe – one of the specialities of the region. Serve with a few slices of toasted ciabatta and a green salad.

Serves 4

2 live lobsters, each about 1kg
1 red onion, peeled and very finely sliced
150ml red wine vinegar
Juice of 1 lemon
8 tablespoons extra virgin olive oil

12 fresh yellow cherry tomatoes, quartered
2 tablespoons chopped fresh flat-leaf parsley
Salt and freshly ground black pepper

1. Make a few air holes in a large plastic bag, place the lobsters in the bag and seal. Transfer immediately to the freezer for 45 minutes.

2. Bring a large saucepan of water to the boil, add the lobsters and cook for about 12 minutes. Lift out with tongs and set aside to cool. Put the onion in a small bowl and pour over the vinegar. Leave to marinate for 20 minutes, then drain.

3. Meanwhile, remove the meat from the lobsters. First twist off the large claws. Using a nutcracker, small hammer or rolling pin, crack the shells of the claws without crushing them. Pick out the meat. Put the meat in a bowl and set aside.

4. Place one lobster body shell on a board, belly-side down. Using a sharp, heavy knife, split the lobster in half lengthways, cutting from the head to the tail. Pull the halves apart. Discard the intestinal tract from the tail and the stomach sac.

5. Remove the meat from the shell (including the greenish-grey liver and any coral-coloured roe). Cut the meat into 2cm chunks and put in the bowl with the claw meat. Retain the shells and remove and discard the legs. Repeat with the second lobster.

6. To make the dressing, put the lemon juice in a medium bowl and gradually whisk in the oil. Season with salt and pepper.

7. Add the lobster meat to the dressing and stir for 1 minute until thoroughly coated. Add the drained onions, tomatoes, parsley and a little salt and pepper. Stir to combine. Spoon the mixture back into the shells, place each half shell on a plate and serve at room temperature.

CHICKEN STEW WITH CAPERS & SAFFRON

Pollo in casseruola con capperi e zafferano

There is something very appealing about chicken stew – a tasty, honest dish with no fuss – and this recipe is made a little bit different by the addition of capers and saffron. If you have time, it's best to joint a whole chicken (and use the carcass to make stock), but ready-jointed chicken pieces are a lot quicker and easier. Serve with warm bread, rice, fregola, potatoes – anything that will soak up the sauce.

Serves 4

1 pinch of saffron threads
8 chicken pieces on the bone (mixture of legs and bone-in
  thighs), about 1.2kg in total, trimmed
6 tablespoons olive oil
1 large red onion, peeled and finely chopped

6 tablespoons small capers, drained
2 tablespoons chopped fresh flat-leaf parsley
250ml hot chicken stock
70ml red wine vinegar
Salt and freshly ground black pepper

1. Put the saffron in a small bowl, add 120ml warm water and set aside.

2. Season the chicken with salt and pepper. Heat the oil in a large flameproof casserole or large saucepan over a medium to high heat. When very hot, add half the chicken, skin-side down, and fry for about 5 minutes each side or until golden brown all over. Transfer to a large plate using a slotted spoon and set aside. Repeat for the remaining chicken.

3. Reduce the heat to medium. Add the onion, capers and parsley to the casserole and fry for 5 minutes, stirring and scraping the bottom of the pan to release any sticky bits left from the chicken.

4. Return the chicken and its juices to the casserole. Pour over the stock, vinegar and saffron mixture and bring to the boil.

5. Reduce the heat, cover and simmer for 35–40 minutes or until the chicken is cooked through and tender and the sauce is thickened, turning the chicken at least 3 times. Season with salt and pepper.

CHICKEN ARRABBIATA WITH PANCETTA & RED WINE

Pollo all'arrabbiata con pancetta e vino rosso

The name 'arrabbiata' comes from the Italian word *la rabbia*, meaning anger, probably referring to the hot, fiery dried chillies in the dish and their possible effect on the diner. If you have any sauce left over, toss it in pasta the following day and another meal is made. Serve with crusty bread to mop up the juices and a green salad.

Serves 4

8 chicken thighs (bone in, skin on), about 1kg in
 total, trimmed
5 tablespoons olive oil
1 large red onion, peeled and finely sliced
250g smoked pancetta, diced
2 tablespoons chopped fresh rosemary

2 teaspoons dried chilli flakes
80ml heavy-bodied red wine (preferably Cannonau)
2 x 400g tins of chopped tomatoes
4 bay leaves
Salt

1. Season the chicken with salt. Heat the oil in a large saucepan or flameproof casserole over a medium to high heat. When very hot, add half the chicken, skin-side down, and fry for about 5 minutes each side or until golden brown all over. Transfer to a large plate using a slotted spoon and set aside. Repeat for the remaining chicken.

2. Reduce the heat to medium. Add the onion and pancetta to the casserole and fry for 5 minutes, stirring and scraping the bottom of the pan to release any sticky bits left from the chicken. Add the rosemary and chilli flakes and fry for 1 minute.

3. Increase the heat and pour in the wine. Bring to the boil and let it bubble rapidly for 1–2 minutes. Add the tomatoes and bay leaves.

4. Return the chicken and its juices to the casserole and bring to the boil. Reduce the heat, cover and simmer for 30 minutes, stirring occasionally.

5. Remove the lid and continue to cook, over a high heat, for about 5 minutes or until the chicken is tender and the sauce has thickened slightly.

RABBIT BRAISED IN MIRTO LIQUEUR & RED WINE

Brasato di coniglio con liquore al mirto e vino rosso

Rabbit has a lovely mild, gamey flavour and firm, meaty texture; if you haven't tried it, I urge you to do so. Ask your butcher to prepare it for you. If you really don't fancy rabbit, chicken pieces make a good substitute. Mirto liqueur is often available in Italian delicatessens or online, but if you can't find it use port or sloe gin instead.

Serves 4

1 rabbit, skinned, gutted, head removed and cut
 into 8 pieces
2 tablespoons flour
6 tablespoons olive oil
60g salted butter
1 red onion, peeled and finely chopped
5 celery hearts, roughly chopped
150ml full-bodied red wine (preferably Cannonau)

2 sprigs of fresh rosemary
2 litres hot chicken stock
Salt and freshly ground black pepper

For the marinade
300ml red mirto liqueur
5 garlic cloves, peeled and lightly crushed
8 bay leaves

1. Put all the ingredients for the marinade in a shallow, non-metallic dish. Add the rabbit and stir to combine. Cover with cling film and refrigerate for 12-24 hours.

2. About 1 hour before cooking, take the dish out of the fridge. Remove the rabbit from the marinade using a slotted spoon and drain well on kitchen paper. Pat the meat dry with more kitchen paper. Put the flour on a large plate and season with salt and pepper. Dip the rabbit in the seasoned flour to coat, shake off any excess and set aside. Reserve the marinade.

3. Heat the oil and butter in a large flameproof casserole over a medium to high heat. When very hot, fry the rabbit in 2 batches until well browned. Transfer to a large plate using a slotted spoon and set aside.

4. Reduce the heat to medium. Add the onion and celery to the casserole and fry for 5 minutes.

5. Increase the heat and pour in the wine. Bring to the boil and let it bubble rapidly for 1-2 minutes. Add the reserved marinade and the rosemary and cook for 5 minutes or until reduced by half. Pour in the stock, season with salt and pepper and bring to the boil.

6. Return the rabbit and its juices to the casserole and bring to the boil. Reduce the heat to low, cover loosely with foil and simmer gently for 2½ hours, turning occasionally. Remove the foil and cook for a further 10 minutes, then transfer the meat to a large plate. Keep warm.

7. Increase the heat to high and boil the sauce for about 30 minutes or until reduced by half. Season with salt and pepper. Reduce the heat and return the rabbit to the pan for 1-2 minutes before serving.

ROASTED SUCKLING PIG WITH CINNAMON-FLAVOURED APPLE SAUCE

Porcheddu con salsa di mele alla cannella

The king of traditional Sardinian dishes, roasted suckling pig is melt-in-your-mouth tender, full of flavour and makes an impressive display. Traditionally a whole pig is cooked very slowly in a pit in the garden with myrtle twigs, but here I have adapted the recipe for a modern domestic oven and used rosemary sprigs instead. Ask your butcher to spatchcock, or flatten, the pig. If you can't source a suckling pig, use belly of pork on the bone instead. Serve with roasted vegetables.

Serves 6

½ suckling pig or 5kg belly of pork on the bone
10 sprigs of fresh rosemary, plus extra to garnish
1 tablespoon coarse sea salt
Freshly ground black pepper

For the sauce
50g salted butter
6 Granny Smith apples, peeled, cored and sliced
50g caster sugar
½ teaspoon ground cinnamon
30ml vermouth (preferably Martini bianco) (optional)

1. Preheat the oven to 220°C/gas mark 7. Place the meat, skin-side up, on a rack in a large roasting tin. Tuck the rosemary under the meat. Rub the salt all over the skin. Leave for 15 minutes.

2. Roast for 30 minutes, then reduce the oven temperature to 160°C/gas mark 3 and cook for a further 1¼ hours. Reduce the temperature to 120°C/gas mark ¼ and roast for a further 40 minutes.

3. Meanwhile, to make the apple sauce place the butter in a medium saucepan over a medium heat. Add the apples and cook for 8 minutes, stirring occasionally. Add the sugar, cinnamon and vermouth (if using), stir and boil for 1 minute.

4. Reduce the heat to low, cover and cook for a further 20 minutes or until soft, stirring occasionally. Transfer to a serving bowl and keep warm.

5. Remove the meat from the oven and increase the temperature to 220°C/gas mark 7. While the oven is heating up, brush all the salt off the skin using a dry, clean cloth.

6. When the oven has reached the required temperature, return the meat to the oven and roast for a further 30 minutes or until the skin is golden and crisp.

7. To serve, place the meat on a large board and carve into 24 large chunks. Arrange the meat on a warm serving platter and garnish with rosemary sprigs. Serve the apple sauce alongside the pork.

WILD BOAR STEW

Spezzatino di cinghiale

Driving back to my house in Sardinia last autumn after a night out with my family, I saw a strange man prowling around on the long winding roads. I stopped and asked him if he was OK and he replied that he was fine, just tracking the wild boar he'd seen earlier that day. Although it may seem a strange way to spend an evening it is not that uncommon in Sardinia, where wild boar is a very popular option on menus. I would suggest you go to your local butcher rather than attempt to catch your own boar, but do try this dish as it's delicious. Serve with plain boiled rice or crusty bread.

Serves 6

900g wild boar for stewing (e.g. neck, shoulder), trimmed and cut into 5cm cubes
3 tablespoons plain flour
6 tablespoons olive oil
1 red onion, peeled and finely chopped
I fresh, medium-hot red chilli, deseeded and finely chopped
4 bay leaves
300ml beef stock
2 large waxy potatoes (preferably Desirée), peeled and cut into 4cm cubes

100g pitted green olives, drained
Salt and freshly ground black pepper

For the marinade
750ml bottle of full-bodied red wine (preferably Cannonau)
1 celery stick, roughly chopped
1 red onion, peeled and roughly chopped
1 large carrot, peeled and roughly chopped
4 sprigs of fresh rosemary

1. Put all the ingredients for the marinade in a large, non-metallic bowl. Add the meat and stir well. Cover with cling film and refrigerate for 12–36 hours.

2. About 1 hour before cooking, take the bowl out of the fridge. Remove the meat from the marinade using a slotted spoon and drain on kitchen paper then pat the meat dry with more kitchen paper. Put the flour in a large bowl and toss the meat in the flour. Strain the marinade, reserving the liquid.

3. Heat the oil in a large, heavy-based saucepan or flameproof casserole over a medium to high heat. When very hot, fry the meat in 3 batches until well browned on all sides. Remove the meat with a slotted spoon and transfer to a bowl.

4. Reduce the heat slightly. Add the onion, chilli and bay leaves to the pan and fry for 2 minutes. Return the meat to the pan with any juices and add the reserved marinade and stock to cover the meat. Stir.

5. Bring to the boil then reduce the heat to low. Simmer, half-covered with a lid, for 1 hour, stirring occasionally. Add the potatoes and olives, season with salt and pepper and cook for 50 minutes or until tender, stirring occasionally.

6. Remove the pan from the heat and set aside to rest for 10 minutes, then serve.

PORK CHOPS IN CRISPY BREADCRUMBS WITH TOMATO SALAD

Cotolette di maiale con insalata di pomodori

This is a perfect dish for a quick mid-week supper or when you have friends over and don't want to spend hours in the kitchen. You can buy breadcrumbs if you haven't got time to make your own, and prepare the salad and get the chops ready for frying several hours ahead. If not frying the chops straightaway, place them on a plate in a single layer and put them in the fridge uncovered so the coating doesn't go soggy.

Serves 6

6 boneless pork chops, trimmed

3 large eggs

200g fine dried breadcrumbs

2 garlic cloves, peeled and finely chopped

3 tablespoons chopped fresh flat-leaf parsley

1 pinch ground saffron (optional)

200ml vegetable oil

6 large fresh basil leaves

Salt and freshly ground black pepper

For the salad

600g fresh ripe plum tomatoes, roughly chopped

1 large red onion, peeled and finely sliced

4 celery hearts, roughly chopped

12 small fresh basil leaves

4 tablespoons extra virgin olive oil

2 tablespoons freshly squeezed lemon juice

1. Beat the chops to 1cm thick using a meat mallet or heavy-based saucepan. Break the eggs into a large bowl, season with salt and pepper and lightly beat. Add the chops and leave to soak for 20 minutes, turning if necessary to ensure they are evenly coated.

2. Meanwhile, make the salad. Place the tomatoes in a large bowl. Add the onion, celery and basil. Pour over the oil and lemon juice, season with salt and pepper and mix well. Cover with cling film until serving time (refrigerate if necessary).

3. Place the breadcrumbs on a large plate or tray and add the garlic, parsley and saffron (if using). Season with salt and pepper and mix well. Remove the chops from the egg, letting the excess drain back into the bowl, and coat the chops with the breadcrumb mixture. Pat the crumbs firmly into the egg.

4. Heat the vegetable oil in a large frying pan over a medium heat. Add the crumbed chops and fry for 2 minutes each side until golden and crispy (you may need to do this in 2 batches). Drain on kitchen paper.

5. To serve, place each chop on a warm plate. Scatter over the cold tomato salad and arrange a basil leaf on top.

T-BONE STEAK WITH SPICY PARSLEY & SUN-DRIED TOMATO SAUCE

Tagliata di manzo con salsa piccante di prezzemolo e pomodori secchi

Parsley is used a lot in Sardinian cooking – in fact, the renowned 18th-century botanist Linnaeus believed that it originated in Sardinia. This spicy parsley and sun-dried tomato sauce goes beautifully with the chargrilled beef, and it is definitely a special occasion dish. Characterised by the T-shaped bone in the cut of the meat, these steaks are the best of both worlds: on one side of the bone is a piece of tender fillet and on the other side a piece of flavoursome sirloin. Serve with warm, crusty bread.

Serves 4

3 T-bone steaks, about 2cm thick
4 tablespoons extra virgin olive oil
70g rocket leaves
Juice of 1 lemon
Salt and freshly ground black pepper

For the sauce
50g fresh flat-leaf parsley
2 garlic cloves, peeled
1 teaspoon dried chilli flakes
3 tablespoons red wine vinegar
100g sun-dried tomatoes in oil, drained
150ml extra virgin olive oil
½ teaspoon salt

1. Preheat a ridged cast-iron chargrill pan over a high heat for 5–10 minutes. Meanwhile, blitz the ingredients for the sauce using a blender or food processor. Pour into a small bowl and set aside.

2. Pat the steaks dry with kitchen paper and brush both sides with the oil. Season with pepper. Lay the steaks in the hot pan. Cook for 2–3 minutes each side for rare to medium rare (cook longer if you like them medium or well done). You will probably have to cook the steaks in 2 batches.

3. Transfer the steaks to a large board, season with salt and pepper and leave to rest for 3 minutes. Slice into strips 1cm wide.

4. To serve, scatter the rocket on a large platter and arrange the sliced steak on top. Squeeze over the lemon juice. Serve immediately with the sauce alongside the beef.

BEEF BRAISED IN CANNONAU WINE

Brasato di manzo al Cannonau

Cannonau is a wonderful, full-bodied Sardinian wine and is well worth seeking out for this recipe as its robust character really complements the beef. Known in Italy as *vino nero* (black wine), research has proved it contains more procyanidins (antioxidants that are most effective in protecting against hardening of the arteries) than any other wine in the world – a fact that could explain the incredible lifespans of the island's inhabitants. So cook this and live long! Serve with Warm Potato Salad (see page 106) or plain rice.

Serves 4

800g beef brisket, trimmed and cut into 3cm cubes
3 tablespoons vegetable oil
750ml bottle of full-bodied red wine (preferably Cannonau)
250ml hot beef stock
2 bay leaves
4 tablespoons olive oil

3 red onions, peeled and each cut into 6 wedges
2 large carrots, halved lengthways and sliced into
  3cm lengths
1 tablespoon fresh thyme leaves
Salt and freshly ground black pepper

1. Season the meat with salt and pepper. Heat the vegetable oil in a large, heavy-based saucepan or flameproof casserole over a medium to high heat. When very hot, fry the meat in 3 batches until well browned on all sides. Return all the meat to the pan.

2. Pour over the wine and bring to the boil. Reduce the heat and simmer for about 15 minutes or until reduced by half, stirring occasionally. Pour over the stock, add the bay leaves and bring to the boil. Reduce the heat, cover and simmer gently for 1½ hours.

3. Heat the olive oil in a large frying pan over a medium heat. Add the onions, carrots and thyme and fry for about 8 minutes or until golden brown, stirring occasionally.

4. Tip the cooked vegetables into the pan with the beef and stir to combine. Replace the lid and simmer for a further 50 minutes or until tender. Add a little hot water if needed.

5. Remove the pan from the hob and leave to rest with the lid on for 15 minutes, then serve.

ROAST LEG OF LAMB STUFFED WITH FRESH HERBS & GARLIC

Coscia di agnello al forno ripiena di erbette ed aglio

This is a very traditional Sardinian recipe that is often made with baby goat – which is beautifully tender with a mild flavour. The boned meat is stuffed with herbs and spices and rolled, so the dish not only looks great when sliced, but the stuffing adds moisture and flavour to the meat during cooking and makes it easier to carve. Ask your butcher to bone the meat for you – it will save you a lot of work.

Serves 4

1 boned leg of lamb, about 1.3kg after boning
2 tablespoons plain flour
5 tablespoons extra virgin olive oil
1 large red onion, peeled and roughly chopped
1 large carrot, peeled and roughly chopped
250ml dry white wine
15g knob salted butter

For the stuffing
10 fresh mint leaves, shredded
2 tablespoons chopped fresh rosemary
6 sage leaves, shredded
1 tablespoon fennel seeds, roughly crushed
3 garlic cloves, finely sliced
Salt and freshly ground black pepper

1. Put all the ingredients for the stuffing in a bowl, stir to combine and set aside. Preheat the oven to 190°C/gas mark 5. Place the meat, skin-side down, on a flat surface. Cover with cling film and, using a meat mallet or heavy-based saucepan, beat until 2cm thick. Take off the cling film, spread over the herb mixture, leaving a small border around the edges, and season.

2. Starting from the narrow end, roll up the meat like a Swiss roll, tucking in the sides at the widest part to create a neat parcel. Tie string around the joint at regular intervals. Dust all over with flour.

3. Heat the oil in a large ovenproof frying pan or flameproof casserole over a medium to high heat. When very hot, brown the meat on all sides, then remove it from the pan, transfer to a large plate and set aside. Reduce the heat to medium. Add the onion and carrot and fry for 5 minutes, stirring occasionally.

4. Return the meat to the pan with any juices, pour in the wine and boil for 2 minutes or until the wine has reduced by half. Pour in 120ml boiling water and loosely cover the pan with foil. Transfer to the oven. After 30 minutes, baste the meat and add another 50ml boiling water. Return to the oven and cook for a further 25 minutes (for medium rare).

5. Remove the meat from the pan and place on a board. Cover loosely with foil and leave in a warm place to rest for 10 minutes. Meanwhile, strain the juices from the pan into a small saucepan, place over a high heat and boil until reduced to a gravy consistency. Stir in any juices from the resting meat, then whisk in the butter. Season with salt and pepper.

6. To serve, remove the string from the meat and carve into slices. Arrange on a warm serving platter and pour over the gravy.

LAMB CASSEROLE WITH FENNEL, MUSHROOMS, CAPERS & HONEY

Agnello al forno con finocchi, funghi, capperi e miele

In Sardinia, sheep are said to outnumber people three to one, so it is no surprise that lamb is often on the menu. There is something so comforting about a lamb casserole, and it tastes even better if you make it a day ahead. The honey and fennel add intriguing sweet and aniseed notes, while the capers give a little piquancy.

Serves 6

3 tablespoons plain flour

900g boned leg of lamb, trimmed and cut into 2cm cubes

6 tablespoons olive oil

1 large onion, peeled and finely sliced

2 fennel bulbs, cored and sliced

100g smoked pancetta, diced

150g chestnut mushrooms, quartered

125ml full-bodied red wine (preferably Cannonau)

450ml hot lamb or beef stock

2 x 400g tins of chopped tomatoes

100g capers, drained and chopped

2 sprigs of fresh rosemary

1 tablespoon runny honey

Salt and freshly ground black pepper

1. Preheat the oven to 160°C/gas mark 3. Place the flour in a large bowl and season with salt and pepper. Pat the cubes of meat dry with kitchen paper and toss in the seasoned flour.

2. Heat the oil in a large flameproof casserole over a medium to high heat. When very hot, fry the meat in 3 batches until well browned on all sides. Remove the meat with a slotted spoon and transfer to a large plate.

3. Reduce the heat to medium. Add the onion, fennel and pancetta and fry for 5 minutes, stirring occasionally, then tip in the mushrooms and fry for 3 minutes. Increase the heat and pour in the wine. Bring to the boil and let it bubble for 2 minutes.

4. Return the meat to the pan. Add the stock, tomatoes, capers, rosemary and honey. Season with salt and pepper. Bring to the boil, stirring. Cover the casserole, transfer it to the oven and cook for 1½ hours. Remove the lid and cook for a further 30 minutes or until the meat is tender.

5. Remove the casserole from the oven and discard the rosemary sprigs. Re-cover and leave to rest at room temperature for 15 minutes, then serve.

SIDE DISHES

Sardinia

SIDE DISHES

The side dishes in Sardinia are simple yet spectacular. The vegetables are so fresh that you could quite easily make a whole meal of them. Artichokes, fennel and beans are popular and a strong-flavoured asparagus is available in spring. The corn on the cob is among the best I've tasted and the mushrooms are also wonderful; they can be cooked in so many ways and provide amazing earthy flavours. Fresh salads are usually kept very simple: lettuce leaves are often served with just a sprinkling of lemon juice; a larger salad may contain a combination of tomatoes, grated carrots, sweetcorn, mozzarella, marinated vegetables and olives.

A speciality of the island is fregola, which looks like large couscous and consists of small balls of semolina pasta. It is served hot or cold, sometimes in a salad of olives, citrus and fresh herbs, or mixed with roasted vegetables, such as courgettes, peppers and onions. Couscous and mixed-bean salads are also very popular and there are countless variations. Another speciality unique to Sardinia is pane carasau – a flatbread shaped into very thin discs and often flavoured with extra virgin olive oil, rosemary and salt. It is also sometimes used in cooked dishes and really is a must-try.

In the Antipasti & Soups chapter you'll find some more vegetable dishes that can be served with the main course, so feel free to 'mix and match' between chapters. The main thing to remember is that as in mainland Italy and Sicily, Sardinians serve side dishes on separate plates rather than on the same plate as the main course. It allows the individual flavours to be enjoyed separately rather than taking on the juices or sauces of the other. So now you know you can not only cook like a Sardinian, but you can serve food like one too!

FREGOLA SALAD WITH OLIVES, ORANGE ZEST & FRESH HERBS

Insalata di fregola con olive, scorza d'arancia ed erbette

A true Sardinian speciality, fregola is a type of pasta typically made from semolina dough. It is similar to couscous, but with larger pellets that have been toasted in the oven so it has a firmer texture and nuttier flavour. You can find fregola of differing sizes in Italian delicatessens and online – it is perfect with fish or shellfish.

Serves 4

160g fregola
7 tablespoons extra virgin olive oil
150g pitted green olives, drained and quartered
1 garlic clove, peeled and finely sliced
1 tablespoon chopped fresh marjoram

10 fresh mint leaves, shredded
Grated zest of 1 large unwaxed orange
3 tablespoons balsamic vinegar
Salt and freshly ground black pepper

1. Bring a large pan of salted water to the boil. Add the fregola and cook for about 8 minutes or until al dente. Drain thoroughly, toss with 3 tablespoons of the oil and spread out on a large plate or tray to cool completely.

2. Meanwhile, put the olives in a large bowl with the garlic, marjoram, mint and orange zest. Add the remaining oil and the vinegar and stir to combine.

3. Fold in the fregola and season with salt and pepper. Toss well. Serve at room temperature.

COUSCOUS SALAD WITH ARTICHOKES, TOMATOES, ALMONDS, OLIVES & CAPERS

Insalata di couscous con carciofi, pomodorini, mandorle, olive e capperi

Sardinia's proximity to Tunisia means that there is a strong North African influence in the food, particularly in the south of the island where Arabic-inspired dishes, often featuring couscous, are prevalent. This salad is wonderful served as a side dish with grilled or barbecued meats and fish, and if you add some roasted vegetables you have a great packed lunch.

Serves 4

250g couscous
350ml hot vegetable stock
6 tablespoons extra virgin olive oil
100g pitted Kalamata olives, drained and halved
2 tablespoons capers, drained and chopped
60g flaked almonds

Grated zest and juice of 3 unwaxed lemons
10 fresh mint leaves, shredded
6 chargrilled artichoke hearts in oil, drained and quartered
20 fresh yellow cherry tomatoes, quartered
Salt and freshly ground black pepper

1. Place the couscous in a large heatproof bowl. Pour over the stock. Cover tightly with cling film and leave for about 10 minutes or until all the stock is absorbed. Fluff up the grains with a fork.

2. Heat half the oil in a frying pan over a medium heat. Add the olives, capers, almonds, lemon zest and mint and fry for 3 minutes. Leave to cool.

3. Add the contents of the frying pan to the couscous. Stir in the artichokes, tomatoes, lemon juice and remaining oil. Toss well to combine. Season with salt and pepper. Serve at room temperature.

CRISP FRIED ARTICHOKES

Carciofi fritti

Globe artichokes are a major crop in Sardinia. Usually, whole baby artichokes are marinated in oil and herbs and served raw, or are boiled and served with salt, but I love this version – coated in semolina and deep-fried. Baby globe artichokes can be hard to get hold of in Britain, but you can buy larger ones and then cut them into pieces. Serve as an accompaniment to fish or as a first course.

Serves 4

3 lemons (2 freshly squeezed, 1 quartered)
12 baby globe artichokes
220g coarse semolina

About 1 litre vegetable oil for deep-frying
Salt and freshly ground black pepper

1. Fill a large bowl with cold water and add the lemon juice and lemon quarters.

2. Peel off the dark outer leaves of each artichoke until you reach the tender light green leaves. Using a sharp knife, cut off the top third of the artichoke and trim the stalk to 2cm long. Gently peel the stalk and use a teaspoon to scoop out the hairy choke from the centre of the artichoke; discard.

3. Rub the artichoke with one of the lemon quarters and immerse it in the acidulated water. Repeat with the remaining artichokes.

4. Cut the artichokes in half lengthways and pat dry with kitchen paper. Place the semolina in a medium bowl and toss the artichokes in the semolina to coat.

5. Heat a deep-fat fryer to 190°C, or heat the oil in a deep pan or a wok until very hot. To test the temperature, add a tiny piece of bread; it will sizzle when the oil is hot enough for frying.

6. Gently lower the artichokes into the hot oil so they are not touching (you will need to fry in batches). Fry for 3 minutes then turn and fry the other side for 2 minutes or until golden and crisp. Drain on kitchen paper and season with salt and pepper. Serve immediately.

BROAD BEANS WITH PANCETTA, THYME & WHITE WINE

Fave con pancetta, timo e vino bianco

A culinary highlight of early summer, broad beans are high in protein and vitamin C and they're also easy to grow. They have a wonderful smooth, creamy texture and perfectly complement the red onion, pancetta and thyme in this dish, while the wine gives depth of flavour. A great accompaniment to meat or can be served as a starter.

Serves 6

2kg fresh young broad beans in the pod or 550g podded
  broad beans
3 tablespoons extra virgin olive oil
1 red onion, peeled and finely chopped

250g smoked pancetta, diced
½ tablespoon chopped fresh thyme
120ml dry white wine (preferably Vermentino)
Salt and freshly ground black pepper

1. Remove the beans from their pods (unless you are using podded beans) and set aside.

2. Heat the oil in a large frying pan over a medium heat. Add the onion and fry for 5 minutes. Sprinkle over the pancetta and thyme and fry for 8 minutes, stirring occasionally.

3. Gently stir in the broad beans and season with salt and pepper. Increase the heat and pour in the wine. Bring to the boil and let it bubble for 2 minutes.

4. Pour over 200ml hot water, reduce the heat to low and simmer for 20 minutes, stirring occasionally. If the beans start to look dry, add a little more water.

5. Just before serving, check for seasoning. Serve hot or at room temperature.

SPICY THREE-BEAN RATATOUILLE

Ratatouille piccante ai tre fagioli

If you're looking for a dish that's packed with flavour to accompany a simple dish, such as grilled meat, this makes a great choice; it can also be served as a main course for vegetarians. Full of protein, fibre and vitamins yet low in fat, beans form a major part of the Sardinian diet and are considered by many to be a key factor in the islanders' remarkable longevity.

Serves 6

6 tablespoons olive oil

1 large red onion, peeled and finely sliced

1 red pepper, deseeded and sliced

1 yellow pepper, deseeded and sliced

1 small aubergine, about 250g, cut into 1cm cubes

2 teaspoons dried chilli flakes

2 x 400g tins of chopped tomatoes

200ml hot vegetable stock

1 x 400g tin of cannellini beans, rinsed and drained

1 x 400g tin of borlotti beans, rinsed and drained

200g fine green beans, trimmed and halved across

3 tablespoons chopped fresh flat-leaf parsley

Salt

1. Heat the oil in a large frying pan over a medium heat. Add the onion and fry for 5 minutes or until softened but not browned. Add the red and yellow peppers and the aubergine, sprinkle over the chilli flakes and fry for 8 minutes, stirring occasionally.

2. Stir in the tomatoes and stock. Simmer gently for 20 minutes, stirring occasionally.

3. Tip in the cannellini and borlotti beans and cook for 5 minutes, then add the green beans and parsley and cook for 8 minutes, stirring occasionally. Season with salt. Serve immediately.

POTATOES BAKED WITH TOMATOES

Patate al forno con pomodorini

In this classic southern Italian dish the humble potato is transformed into something really wonderful. It is best made in summer, when tomatoes are in season and bursting with flavour. The perfect dish for entertaining, you can prepare it ahead and easily double the quantities if you're cooking for more people. If you have any leftovers, chop them up and toss in some eggs to make a delicious frittata for lunch.

Serves 4

8 tablespoons extra virgin olive oil

500g maincrop potatoes (preferably Désirée), peeled
 and thinly sliced

1 teaspoon dried oregano

20 fresh basil leaves

1 large red onion, peeled and finely sliced

500g fresh red cherry tomatoes, halved and deseeded

2 tablespoons dry white wine

Salt and freshly ground black pepper

1. Preheat the oven to 190°C/gas mark 5. Spread half the oil over the bottom of a baking dish measuring about 30 x 20cm.

2. Layer half the potato slices in the dish, slightly overlapping. Sprinkle over half the oregano and half the basil. Season with salt and pepper. Scatter over half the onion and half the tomatoes. Repeat the layers once more. Finally, pour over the remaining oil and the wine.

3. Cover the dish with foil and bake for 40 minutes. Remove the foil and bake for a further 15 minutes or until golden brown. Serve immediately.

WARM POTATO SALAD WITH CARAMELISED ONIONS & ITALIAN BEER

Insalata calda di patate con cipolle caramellate e birra

In Italy, we tend to make potato salad with an oil and vinegar dressing instead of mayonnaise, which can sometimes be a little too rich and cloying. For this recipe, I decided to replace the vinegar with Italian beer, which adds depth to the dish without being overpowering. Make sure you use lager (ideally Italian), as darker ale will discolour the potatoes and be too strong. To accompany any fish or meat dish.

Serves 6

1kg maincrop potatoes (preferably Désirée), scrubbed
6 tablespoons extra virgin olive oil
3 large red onions, peeled and finely sliced

250ml Italian beer (lager)
2 tablespoons chopped fresh flat-leaf parsley
Salt and freshly ground black pepper

1. Place the unpeeled whole potatoes in a large saucepan and cover with cold salted water. Bring to the boil and simmer for about 35 minutes (depending on size) or until a skewer can be inserted without any resistance. Drain well.

2. When the potatoes are cool enough to handle, peel and cut into slices 1cm thick. Arrange on a serving platter, overlapping the slices slightly, and set aside.

3. Heat the oil in a large frying pan over a medium to low heat. Add the onions, season with salt and pepper and fry for 15 minutes or until softened and brown, stirring occasionally.

4. Increase the heat and pour over the beer. Bring to the boil and let it bubble until most of the liquid has evaporated, stirring constantly. Spoon the onions with any remaining liquid over the potatoes. Scatter over the parsley and serve warm.

SARDINIAN FLATBREAD

Pane carasau

The traditional bread of Sardinia, pane carasau is paper-thin and very crisp – almost like a large cracker or poppadum. The recipe was originally created for shepherds, who were away from home for long periods and needed a type of bread that would not go mouldy; if stored in an airtight container, it can last up to 4 months. Pane carasau is sometimes soaked or dipped in stock, water or other liquid to soften and is used in several Sardinian dishes (see pages 31 and 65).

Makes 24

1kg strong white flour, plus extra for dusting

3g fast-action (easy blend) dried yeast

4 teaspoons fine sea salt

1. Place the flour in a large bowl. Add the yeast to one side of the bowl and the salt to the other. Make a well in the centre and gradually pour in 480ml warm water. Mix together using the handle of a wooden spoon to create a soft dough. Knead the dough on a lightly floured surface for about 10 minutes or until smooth and elastic.

2. Cut the dough into 12 equal-sized pieces and shape each piece into a ball. Place the balls spaced well apart on 2 large, lightly floured baking sheets. Cover with a tea towel and leave to rest in a warm place for 1½ hours or until doubled in size.

3. Dust the work surface and a sheet of greaseproof paper lightly with flour. Roll out one of the balls into a thin disc, about 10–15cm diameter and 2mm thick, and lay it on the greaseproof paper. Dust the top of the flatbread with a little flour.

4. Lay a new sheet of greaseproof paper on top and continue as before until all the flatbreads are rolled out and stacked with a flour-dusted sheet of paper between each one. Leave to rise in a warm place for 1 hour.

5. Meanwhile, preheat the oven to 220°C/gas mark 7. Place a 30 x 30cm terracotta tile on the middle shelf of the oven until hot (alternatively, use a pizza stone or baking sheet).

6. Turn the stack of flatbreads upside down, so the one you rolled first is now on top. Gently slide the top flatbread onto the hot terracotta tile and immediately close the oven. Within 1 minute it should puff up. If it doesn't, return the stack of remaining flatbreads to a warm place to rest for a further 30 minutes.

7. Remove the puffed flatbread from the oven using a fish slice and place it on a board. While still hot, use a serrated knife to split it horizontally across the centre and peel it apart so you now have 2 flatbreads. Place the top half of the flatbread on top of the bottom half and immediately place a wooden board on top to weigh them down. Repeat with the remaining flatbreads, stacking one on top of the other beneath the board.

8. Turn the stack over again and place the top flatbread back on the terracotta tile in the oven. Bake for 2 minutes until pale and golden.

DESSERTS

Sardinia

DESSERTS

Sardinian cuisine is remarkably varied throughout the island – particularly given its size – and desserts, or dolci, are no exception.

Generally, the desserts are a lot less creamy in Sardinia than in mainland Italy, and while you will find tiramisu and profiteroles on most menus I really recommend you try the local favourites. One of the great traditional Sardinian desserts is seadas (sometimes called sebadas) – deep-fried pastries filled with fresh pecorino (local sheep's cheese) and covered with honey. The combination of sweet honey and salty cheese is out of this world. Honey is fantastic in Sardinia and the various flavours just have to be explored: try a simple piece of fresh fruit topped with honey – perfection; it never ceases to amaze me how no two types of honey ever seem to taste the same on the island.

Almonds are used a lot in Sardinian cakes, biscuits and pastries and they're the star attraction in torrone – a type of nougat. Fresh fruit also makes appearances in many desserts – both in their natural state and cooked. Figs, lemons, oranges, pears, melons, pomegranates, apricots, grapes and many other fruits all flourish in the Sardinian soil and climate and are an important part of the islanders' diet.

If you're travelling around Sardinia you may well be a little confused with the desserts on the menu as they often have local names for a very similar dish – so what is called one thing in one village can be named quite differently in another. However, whatever you choose is more than likely to be absolutely delicious!

PEARS POACHED IN RED WINE WITH GINGER SEMI-FREDDO

Pere al vino rosso con semifreddo allo zenzero

Poached pears make a delicious dessert, particularly paired with this ginger semi-freddo – not only is it a great flavour combination, but the ruby-red colour of the pears looks stunning. I like to poach pears in Cannonau, which is a strong red Sardinian wine that has to be stored in oak barrels for at least a year. However, if you can't find Cannonau, any fruity strong-bodied red wine will be fine. It's best to avoid really soft pears for this dish as they may fall apart when poached.

Serves 6

6 large pears
750ml bottle of full-bodied red wine (preferably Cannonau)
8 cloves
1 cinnamon stick, broken in half
350g caster sugar

For the semi-freddo
150g caster sugar
6 large egg yolks, beaten
200ml double cream
1 teaspoon freshly grated ginger

1. To make the semi-freddo, put the sugar in a small saucepan with 150ml water. Heat over a low heat for several minutes until the sugar has dissolved, stirring occasionally. Increase the heat and bring to the boil. Boil for about 1 minute. Reduce the heat and simmer for 3 minutes, stirring continuously.

2. Whisk the egg yolks in a large bowl then add the syrup mixture in a steady stream, stirring continuously. Once all the sugar has been incorporated continue to whisk until the mixture has cooled slightly (to hand-hot temperature).

3. Place the cream in a large bowl and whip until thick enough to just hold its shape and form soft peaks, then fold in the ginger. Gently fold the ginger cream into the cooled egg mixture in 3 batches. Pour the mixture into a rigid, 1-litre freezerproof container. Cover and freeze for 8 hours.

4. Trim the base of the pears and peel them, leaving the stalks intact. Arrange upright in a medium saucepan (they should fit snugly in a single layer).

5. Add the wine, cloves, cinnamon and sugar. Bring to the boil then cover the pears with a sheet of greaseproof paper weighed down with a small plate. Reduce the heat and simmer for 30 minutes. Lift the pears out of the pan using a slotted spoon, transfer to a large plate, cover and set aside in a warm place.

6. Return the wine to a medium heat and boil for 35 minutes until reduced to a syrup consistency. Leave to cool completely.

7. Take the semi-freddo out of the freezer 10 minutes before serving. To serve, place a pear (warm or room temperature) on a plate, drizzle over the cooled wine syrup and serve with a scoop or two of semi-freddo.

STRAWBERRY, MASCARPONE & PUFF PASTRY STACK WITH HONEY

Torretta di pasta frolla con fragole, mascarpone e miele

When I was in Orgosolo, in eastern-central Sardinia, I visited the Agriturismo Supramonte, where I met a shepherd called Martino. He explained to me how much the island's inhabitants – especially the shepherds – value honey, as it gives them the energy they need for their very physical lives, walking many miles each day. For this reason, they use honey in many savoury as well as sweet dishes. Martino, my dear friend – this recipe is dedicated to you.

Serves 4

350g ready-rolled puff pastry
40g icing sugar, plus extra for dusting
80ml double cream
180g mascarpone cheese

2 tablespoons runny honey, plus extra for drizzling
500g medium strawberries, green stalks removed and halved

1. Preheat the oven to 220°C/gas mark 6. Cut the pastry into 4 circles each about 8cm in diameter. Place the discs on a baking sheet lined with baking parchment and refrigerate for 15 minutes.

2. Turn the discs over and dust with icing sugar. Bake for 6 minutes. Remove from the oven and leave to cool, then carefully slice each pastry disc horizontally to make 3 discs.

3. Put the cream, mascarpone and honey in a medium bowl. Mix to combine and set aside.

4. Place one of the pastry discs on a serving plate. Spread 1 tablespoonful of the mascarpone mixture over the surface, then arrange some strawberries on top, cut-side up, in a single layer. Place another pastry disc on top and repeat the process with the mascarpone mixture and strawberries. Top with the remaining disc of pastry. Repeat for the remaining pastry stacks.

5. To serve, drizzle over some runny honey and dust with icing sugar.

BAKED FRESH FRUITS WITH SARDINIAN GRAPPA

Frutta fresca al forno con Filo e Ferru

During the filming for the TV series I met Carlo Pische, the owner of the Lussurgesi distillery in Oristano, western Sardinia. Carlo produces a delicious grappa called Filu e Ferru and I was so impressed with the product I asked him to suggest a simple recipe using it. He told me that roasted fruits and Filu e Ferru are a match made in heaven – and he's right. If you can't find Filu e Ferru, use any grappa or your favourite liqueur, such as amaretto or Cointreau. Serve with a shot of Filu e Ferru on the side.

Serves 4

8 figs, halved
2 pears, cored, peeled and quartered lengthways
2 plums, halved and stoned

2 peaches, quartered and stoned
Juice of 2 oranges
4 tablespoons Filu e Ferru or other grappa

1. Preheat the oven to 200°C/gas mark 6. Place the figs, pears, plums and peaches cut-side up in a single layer in a roasting tin. Pour over the orange juice and roast for 18 minutes.

2. Remove the tin from the oven and pour the Filu e Ferru over the fruits. Bake for a further 5 minutes. Serve warm.

CHEESE-FILLED FRITTERS WITH HONEY

Seadas

It's virtually impossible to visit a Sardinian restaurant and not find seadas on the menu. Traditionally, women would make these deep-fried cheese pastries for their husbands or fathers returning in spring from their shepherding and they would dress up before presenting them. Seal the edge really well so you don't lose the filling.

Makes 18

500g ricotta cheese
60g sultanas
1 large egg yolk
110g caster sugar
Grated zest of 2 unwaxed lemons
About 1 litre vegetable oil for deep-frying
150ml runny honey

For the dough
500g strong white flour
1 pinch of salt
50g lard (room temperature), cut into cubes

1. Wrap the ricotta in a piece of muslin and place in a sieve set over a medium bowl. Chill for 2 hours. Place the sultanas in a bowl, cover with warm water and leave to soak for 30 minutes. Drain and set aside.

2. To make the dough, place the flour and salt in a large bowl. Add the lard and rub together until you have incorporated all the lard. Make a well in the centre, pour in 200ml warm water and mix using the handle of a wooden spoon. Knead the dough on a lightly floured surface for 10 minutes. Shape into a ball, wrap in cling film and chill for 30 minutes.

3. Meanwhile, remove the muslin from the ricotta, set a sieve over a large bowl and push the ricotta through the sieve using a wooden spoon or spatula. Whisk in the egg yolk, then the sugar and lemon zest. Fold in the sultanas. Set aside.

4. Cut the dough into two equal-sized pieces. Flatten the dough with the palm of your hand then roll out as thinly as possible using a floured rolling pin.

5. Lay the dough on a lightly floured surface. Cut out 36 rounds with a 10cm plain cutter. Place 2 tablespoons of the ricotta mixture in the centre of 18 rounds and cover the filling with the remaining rounds. Press around the edges of each 'parcel' to seal. Transfer the parcels to a lightly floured tray.

6. Heat a deep-fat fryer to 160°C or heat the oil in a deep pan or wok until very hot. To test the temperature, add a tiny piece of dough; it will sizzle when the oil is hot enough for frying.

7. Gently lower the pastries into the hot oil, 6 at a time so they are not touching. Fry without moving for 4 minutes, then turn and fry for a further 2 minutes or until golden and crisp. Remove with a slotted spoon, drain on kitchen paper and keep warm until you have fried all the pastries.

8. Heat the honey in a small saucepan over a low heat. To serve, place 3 hot pastries in the middle of each plate and drizzle over the warm honey.

CATALAN-STYLE, NO-BAKE CRÈME BRÛLÉE

Crema catalana

Custard puddings are very popular in Spain, and given Sardinia was under Spanish rule for about 400 years and the island's proximity to the Catalan coast it is not surprising that the Sardinians have taken them to their hearts too. Crema Catalana is closely related to Spanish flan and French crème brûlée, but you don't need to bake it and the texture is a little more pudding-like. It's perfect for when you want an impressive yet light dessert after a large meal.

Serves 6

4 large egg yolks
2 teaspoons cornflour
200g caster sugar
500ml full-fat milk

1 cinnamon stick
Pinch of saffron threads
1 teaspoon vanilla extract
120g Demerara sugar

1. Place the egg yolks, cornflour and 150g of the caster sugar in a large heatproof bowl. Using an electric hand whisk or a balloon whisk, beat until the mixture is pale and smooth.

2. Pour the milk into a medium saucepan. Add the remaining caster sugar and the cinnamon, saffron and vanilla. Gently bring the milk to a simmer. Remove the pan from the heat just before it comes to the boil, at the point where you can see tiny bubbles appearing around the edge of the pan. Leave to cool slightly for about 2 minutes. Discard the cinnamon stick.

3. Pour the hot milk over the egg mixture in a steady stream, whisking all the time until smooth.

4. Transfer the custard to a clean medium saucepan and place over a low heat. Cook very gently for about 5 minutes, stirring constantly with a wooden spoon, until it thickens enough to coat the back of the spoon.

5. Carefully pour the custard into 6 x 100ml ramekins, leave to cool completely then refrigerate for at least 5 hours or overnight.

6. When ready to serve, sprinkle the Demerara sugar evenly over the tops of the custards.

7. Use a blowtorch to caramelise the sugar, being careful not to burn it. Hold it a few inches above the sugar, and as soon as the sugar melts and turns golden brown in one spot move it to another immediately. If you don't have a blowtorch, preheat the grill to its highest setting and place the ramekins as close to the grill as possible until the sugar caramelises. Remove from the grill and leave to cool for 5 minutes before serving.

SAFFRON & POTATO DOUGHNUTS WITH VODKA & ORANGE

Frisciolas

Carnival celebrations in Sardinia wouldn't be the same without frisciolas – these delicious little saffron-flavoured doughnuts made from potatoes and dusted with orange-flavoured sugar. You can substitute the orange zest for lemon or lime zest, and amaretto and Cointreau work well instead of vodka if you prefer. Perfect with espresso.

Makes about 30

1 medium maincrop potato (preferably Desirée), scrubbed
130ml full-fat milk
Pinch of saffron threads
18g fast-action (easy blend) dried yeast
250g caster sugar
450g plain white flour, plus extra for dusting

1 teaspoon salt
Grated zest and juice of 2 unwaxed oranges
1 medium egg, lightly beaten
50ml vodka
About 1 litre vegetable oil for deep-frying, plus extra
  for greasing

1. Put the potato in a small saucepan and cover with cold salted water. Bring to the boil and simmer for 15–20 minutes or until tender. Drain well and leave for 2–3 minutes to cool slightly, then peel and pass the flesh through a potato ricer set over a plate or bowl. Alternatively, mash using a potato masher until really smooth. Spread out to cool and set aside.

2. Heat the milk and saffron in a small saucepan over a medium heat until just simmering. Remove from the heat. Add the yeast and a pinch of the sugar and whisk until the yeast is thoroughly dissolved. Set aside for 10 minutes.

3. Put the flour and salt in a large bowl. Make a well in the centre and add the orange juice, egg, mashed potato, milk mixture and vodka. Mix together using the handle of wooden spoon.

4. Knead the dough on a lightly floured surface for 5–8 minutes or until soft. Add a little more flour if the dough is too sticky to handle.

5. Shape the dough into a round and place in a large, oiled bowl. Brush a little more oil over the top. Cover with cling film and leave in a warm place for 2 hours.

6. Dust a large tray with flour. Flour your hands and break off walnut-sized pieces of dough and roll into balls. Place the balls on the tray and cover with cling film. Leave in a warm place for 20 minutes. Meanwhile, combine the remaining sugar and orange zest in a shallow tray or on a large plate and set aside.

7. Heat a deep-fat fryer to 160°C or heat the oil in a deep pan or wok until very hot. To test the temperature, add a tiny piece of dough; it will sizzle when the oil is hot enough for frying.

8. Lower the dough balls into the hot oil, 4 or 5 at a time. Fry without moving for 2 minutes, then turn and fry for a further 2 minutes or until golden and crisp. Remove with a slotted spoon and drain on kitchen paper. Toss immediately in the orange-flavoured sugar. Keep warm until you have fried all the balls.

SARDINIAN NOUGAT

Torrone sardo

Nougat is sold in the street markets in most towns in Sardinia and the variations on offer are vast. The one I have chosen to feature in this book is the classic and most popular version and, in my opinion, the best. You can store it in an airtight container for up to a week, but don't put it in the fridge as it will become soft and very sticky.

Makes about 30 pieces

4 sheets edible wafer paper
1 large egg white
1 pinch of salt

320g caster sugar
190g good-quality runny honey
300g unpeeled almonds

1. Lay 2 sheets of wafer paper, slightly overlapping, on a large tray or baking sheet to form a rectangle measuring 24 x 15cm.

2. Put the egg white in a large heatproof bowl and add the salt. Whisk using an electric hand whisk on full speed until the whites stand in stiff peaks.

3. Place the sugar, honey and 2 tablespoons of water in a medium saucepan and heat until it reaches 130°C on a cooking thermometer. Alternatively, if you don't have a thermometer, to test the temperature take a small teaspoon of the sugar mixture, drop it into a small bowl filled with ice water and leave for 2 seconds. The sugar should form hard but pliable threads that bend before cooling completely and breaking.

4. Gradually pour the sugar mixture over the egg white and beat immediately with the electric whisk on low speed. Once all the mixture is added, increase the speed and whisk until it almost doubles in volume. Fold in the almonds and immediately pour all the mixture onto the centre of the wafer paper rectangle. Top with the remaining 2 sheets of wafer paper, slightly overlapping them as before.

5. Using a rolling pin, gently roll over the top sheets of the wafer paper, spreading out the nougat layer beneath evenly until it is about 1cm thick. Leave to cool at room temperature.

6. Trim the edges of the paper. Cut the nougat into 30 pieces using a sharp knife. To make the cutting easier, dip a sharp knife in hot water.

SICILY

Trapani

Palermo

Marsala

Agrigento

STRAIT
OF SICILY

TYRRHENIAN SEA

MAINLAND ITALY

Messina

Savoca

STRAIT OF MESSINA

Taormina

Mt. Etna

Catania

Syracuse

Noto

Modica

ABOUT SICILY

The largest and one of the most populated islands in the Mediterranean, Sicily is the 'football' to Italy's 'boot', lying to the southwest of the mainland and northeast of Tunisia. It is home to the famous Mount Etna, the largest active volcano in Europe, and is very mountainous – skiers love it. If you're interested in visiting historical sites you couldn't choose a better place: there are many ancient temples, amphitheatres and churches ... even mummies. And when it's time to relax, you have a choice between beautiful black or white sandy beaches.

Sicily became part of the Kingdom of Italy in 1861, but before that many tried to claim it as their own – the Greeks, Phoenicians, Romans, Vandals, Byzantines, Arabs, Germans, Normans and Spanish all invaded and left their mark on the culture of this fascinating island – yet, like Sardinia, it still retains a strong identity. Sicilians often have a darker complexion than many mainland Italians, reflecting the presence of Phoenician and Arab ancestry among the island's population – and the Sicilian dialect is so strong that some linguists have argued that it should be classified as a separate language altogether. The people can sometimes be quite formal, unlike the more easy-going southern Italians; this is attributed to the fact that their history has caused them to be a little guarded, making them sometimes appear stand-offish or cold – but please persevere and, believe me, the traditional cuddly mama will emerge!

One part of Sicilian life still very much at the centre of its culture is an organisation dating back to the Middle Ages – the Mafia, of course – and this is probably why traditional bonds of loyalty remain strong there. Even today, the organisation influences certain parts of the island; it is almost as though there were two governments running alongside each other – one legitimate, the other more of a social and political network, maintaining its power through violence. Tourists will rarely be affected by any outbreaks of this violence – it tends to happen in poorer parts of town and invariably affects locals rather than visitors.

While Sicilians did not welcome invaders to their island, there were certainly some benefits, particularly in the area of food. The Phoenicians brought grapes, the Greeks olives, the Romans pasta and pulses, and in the Middle Ages the Arabs introduced artichokes, apricots, aniseed, oranges, pistachios, pomegranates, rice, spinach and saffron; they also passed on their advanced farming and irrigation techniques, methods for drying pasta, and used the snow from the mountains to create granitas and ice cream. Next came the Normans, with their techniques for air-salting fish and their rotating skewers for cooking meat, followed by the Spanish who brought tomatoes, corn, potatoes and chocolate that they had discovered in the New World. All these influences have made a positive mark on the cuisine that still exists to this day – a taste of Sicily is like a taste of everywhere.

Like the Sardinians, Sicilians respect the quality of raw ingredients and food preparation is kept simple. As you might expect, Sicily has fabulous fresh fish and shellfish, which forms the major part of the islanders' diet. Goat, lamb, veal and pork are the preferred meats and cheese is usually made from goat's or sheep's milk. Although the island's main economy is based on the natural gas and sulphur it produces (other industries include salt extraction and shipbuilding), the region still remains mainly agricultural, with much of the land turned over to crops.

Sicilian cuisine certainly has plenty of surprises – bread is topped with sesame seeds, raisins turn up in spaghetti and ice cream is eaten stuffed in a brioche bun for breakfast. Unlike in northern Italy, cream and butter are hardly ever used; instead, Sicilians usually substitute them with olive oil. The cuisine is very exotic and contains many spices, which are – of course – reminders of the island's Arabic heritage. The roots of much Italian cuisine can be found in Sicily, but whereas on mainland Italy cooking techniques have become more modern, in Sicily – as in Sardinia – the traditional methods still hold sway. Sicily is perhaps most renowned for its sweets and fine desserts, and if you visit Palermo you'll come across some of the best patisseries in the world.

As well as the celebrated Marsala, many wonderful wines are produced on the island and it is said that even Julius Caesar praised Sicilian wine. Fantastic white wines are produced around the city of Alcamo, and the new wine-makers on Mount Etna make an award-winning Bordeaux-style red. Wine resorts are now all the rage; here you can taste the wines while learning how to cook traditional Sicilian dishes, which makes for a fantastic holiday. *A saluti*, as they say in Sicily!

ANTIPASTI & SOUPS

Sicily

ANTIPASTI & SOUPS

As in mainland Italy, Sicilian meals start with the antipasti – a splendid array of dishes that whet the appetite with their incredible combination of flavours, aromas and textures. I always think that there is something wonderful about sharing plates of food with others – the informality of tucking into the same dishes seems to relax people and strengthen bonds between friends and family.

Fresh produce is abundant in Sicily, so the quality of the ingredients is excellent. The selection of antipasti served varies according to the season and even the local area. Vegetables are a key part of the antipasti spread: artichokes, tomatoes, beans, olives, aubergines, fennel and peppers are all favourites, served in numerous ways – marinated, stuffed, roasted, grilled or simply sliced and eaten raw in salads. Fruit also makes an appearance in salads, especially melons and oranges.

Of course, fish antipasti are common too – there are marinated fresh anchovies, smoked mackerel salad and thin marinated slices of raw fish – all of which get the taste buds going. Soups are usually vegetable-based and often contain pulses enhanced with fabulous spices. Platters of meat and cheese are also plentiful.

A key difference between Sicilian and Sardinian antipasti is the street food in Sicily. These 'fast food' snacks include arancini (rice croquettes usually stuffed with cheese or ragù), panelle (chickpea fritters) and grilled or barbecued prawn skewers. I visited some amazing places in Palermo, such as the Vucciria street market and the Antica Focacceria San Francesco, where I tried the Palermitano delicacy of a spleen sandwich – and very good it was too. At home, these street-food-style dishes are ideal served at a party – they are the perfect finger food to hold with a drink in hand – but you can also offer them with other antipasti dishes at the table.

Many of the antipasti options in this chapter can double up as side dishes, and vice versa. There are also several dishes in the Main Courses chapter that can be served as antipasti, including the seafood salad, grilled sardines and frittata. In fact, the selection is so diverse you could plan a whole meal around antipasti alone – pick between six and ten dishes, adjust quantities according to the number of guests, serve with some warm, crusty bread and the meal becomes a veritable banquet!

CANTALOUPE MELON, ARTICHOKE & WALNUT SALAD

Insalata di melone, carciofi e noci

This is one of those first-course salads that looks so impressive yet can be prepared in about 15 minutes. It goes perfectly with cold meats and fish dishes but will do any selection of antipasti justice. Substitute the walnuts with pine nuts if you prefer. Accompany with crusty bread.

Serves 4

1 cantaloupe melon
175g chargrilled artichoke hearts in oil, drained and
  roughly chopped
50g walnuts, roughly chopped
70g rocket leaves

For the dressing
Juice of 1 lime
2 tablespoons red wine vinegar
1 tablespoon runny honey
4 tablespoons extra virgin olive oil
Salt and freshly ground black pepper

1. Cut the melon in half, then remove and discard the seeds. Cut into wedges, then carefully remove the peel by running a knife between the flesh and skin. Cut the flesh into 2cm chunks and place in a large bowl. Add the artichokes, walnuts and rocket.

2. To make the dressing, put the lime juice, vinegar and honey in a small bowl. Gradually add the oil, whisking vigorously as you go, and season with salt and pepper. Pour the dressing over the salad and toss together to mix.

SWEET & SOUR PEPPERS WITH RAISINS, PINE NUTS AND CAPERS

Peperonata agrodolce con uvetta passa, pinoli e capperi

Peperonata is a typical dish in Sicily. Peppers were introduced to the island by the Spanish, who brought them from the New World in the late 15th century. The variations of peperonata recipes are endless, but this is my favourite. Serve as part of your antipasti or simply accompanied with warm, crusty bread. Perfect to enjoy cold the following day as a packed lunch.

Serves 4

1 red pepper
1 green pepper
1 yellow pepper
1 orange pepper
4 tablespoons olive oil
1 red onion, peeled and thinly sliced
50g pine nuts

50g raisins
50g capers, drained
100ml white wine vinegar
1 teaspoon runny honey
6 fresh mint leaves, roughly chopped
Salt and freshly ground black pepper

1. Halve and deseed all the peppers and cut them into 2cm chunks.

2. Heat the oil in a large frying pan with a lid or a sauté pan over a medium heat. Add the peppers and onion and fry for 6 minutes or until softened, stirring frequently.

3. Stir in the pine nuts, raisins and capers and fry for 1 minute. Add the vinegar and honey, stir again and bring to the boil. Reduce the heat to low, cover and cook for 15 minutes, stirring occasionally.

4. Just before serving, add the mint and season with salt and pepper.

MARINATED FRESH ANCHOVIES

Acciughe marinate

They might be small, but anchovies pack a huge punch in flavour. This recipe marinates these beautiful fish in wine vinegar, which is typical in Sicily, and with the addition of chilli and capers it makes a really lively, piquant first course. Serve with a little salad of your choice and lots of warm, crusty bread.

Serves 8

700g fresh anchovies, scaled, gutted and filleted
2 tablespoons salt
400ml white wine vinegar
2 garlic cloves, peeled and finely sliced

½ teaspoon dried chilli flakes
20g capers, drained
3 tablespoons chopped fresh flat-leaf parsley
200ml extra virgin olive oil

1. Rinse the anchovies under cold running water and pat dry with kitchen paper. Lay in a single layer in a shallow, non-metallic dish. Sprinkle with the salt and pour over the vinegar. Gently tilt the dish so the vinegar and salt are distributed between the fish. Cover with cling film and refrigerate for 24 hours, turning occasionally.

2. Drain the anchovies and discard the vinegar and salt marinade. Pat the fillets dry with kitchen paper.

3. Arrange the anchovies on a large serving platter. Scatter over the garlic, chilli flakes, capers and parsley. Drizzle over the oil, cover with cling film and return to the fridge for 30 minutes before serving.

SMOKED MACKEREL, ORANGE & FENNEL SALAD

Insalata di sgombro affumicato con arance e finocchi

Oranges go perfectly with smoked mackerel, particularly the red oranges that are so abundant in Sicily. Orange and fennel are a popular combination in Sicilian cuisine, especially in the city of Palermo, and with the addition of this seductively rich-tasting fish this salad becomes the star of any antipasti table.

Serves 6

3 oranges (preferably red or blood oranges)
1 fennel bulb, cored and thinly sliced
1 red onion, peeled and thinly sliced
30g pitted black olives, halved
2 celery sticks, thinly sliced
30g pine nuts
2 smoked mackerel fillets, about 200g in total, skinned
Freshly ground black pepper

For the dressing
2 tablespoons red wine vinegar
1 tablespoon runny honey
6 tablespoons extra virgin olive oil
Salt

1. First peel and segment the oranges. Using a sharp knife, cut off about 1–2cm from the top and bottom of the fruit. Place the fruit on one of its flat ends and cut down to remove the skin and the white pith. Rotate and repeat, working your way around the fruit until the flesh is completely exposed.

2. Working over a large bowl, cut between the flesh and the white membrane to free the segments. Discard the membrane and put the segments into the bowl (the bowl should also catch the juice).

3. Add the fennel, onion, olives, celery and pine nuts to the bowl with the orange segments and juice. Stir carefully to combine.

4. To make the dressing, put the vinegar and honey in a small bowl. Gradually add the oil, whisking vigorously as you go, and season with salt.

5. Pour the dressing over the salad (reserving 1 tablespoon for drizzling) and gently toss all the salad ingredients together.

6. Break the mackerel into bite-sized pieces and scatter over the top of the salad. Sprinkle with black pepper and drizzle over the remaining dressing.

GRILLED PRAWN & SWEET PEPPER SKEWERS WITH SALSA

Spiedini di gamberi e peperoni alla siciliana

This recipe reminds me of being a child playing in the garden when the barbecue was in action. Prawns were always part of our diet and these sticks of gorgeousness were easy to prepare and wonderfully portable. We'd sit under a tree, skewer in hand, and delight in my grandfather's cooking skills. In Sicily, these are cooked on an open grill and served as street food. Here I have adapted the recipe for a domestic grill.

Serves 6

24 raw, peeled king prawns, deveined
1 yellow pepper, deseeded and cut into 24 chunks
1 red pepper, deseeded and cut into 24 chunks
1 large red onion, peeled and cut into 24 chunks
4 tablespoons olive oil
Grated zest of 1 unwaxed lemon
50g fresh white breadcrumbs
Salt and freshly ground black pepper

For the salsa
250g fresh ripe tomatoes, finely chopped
4 tablespoons chopped fresh flat-leaf parsley
10 fresh basil leaves, shredded
6 tablespoons extra virgin olive oil
Juice of 1 lemon
½ teaspoon caster sugar
½ teaspoon salt

1. Soak 6 wooden skewers, about 30cm long, in cold water for at least 30 minutes. Remove the grill rack and line the grill pan with foil.

2. Thread a prawn onto a skewer followed by a piece each of yellow and red pepper, then onion. Repeat until you have 4 of each item on the skewer. Preheat the grill for 5 minutes on its highest setting.

3. Put the oil and lemon zest in a small bowl. Brush the mixture over the skewered prawns and vegetables. Put the breadcrumbs on a plate, dip in the skewers to coat and season with salt and pepper.

4. Arrange the skewers in the grill pan and grill for about 3 minutes each side or until the prawns are cooked through.

5. Meanwhile, put all the ingredients for the salsa in a small mixing bowl and stir to combine.

6. To serve, place the skewers on a large serving platter. Spoon over some of the salsa and serve the rest on the side.

CHICKPEA FRITTERS

Panelle

Chickpea fritters are a hugely popular street food in Palermo. When I was filming for the TV series I tried them at the Antica Focacceria San Francesco, and I can tell you that they are extremely addictive and one is never enough! Make sure you roll out the dough thinly enough – any thicker than 5mm and they will not crisp up. You will find chickpea flour, or gram flour, in some large supermarkets and Asian stores.

Serves 8

500g chickpea (gram) flour
1 tablespoon salt
1 teaspoon freshly ground black pepper

1 tablespoon chopped fresh flat-leaf parsley
About 1 litre vegetable oil for deep-frying

1. Place the flour, salt, pepper and parsley in a bowl and mix together.

2. Put 1.5 litres cold water in a large saucepan and slowly tip the flour mixture into the water, whisking continuously with a balloon whisk. Place over a medium heat and cook, stirring continuously, for 15 minutes or until the mixture has the consistency of a very thick cheese sauce or thick polenta.

3. Pour the thickened mixture onto a sheet of greaseproof paper and cover with another sheet of greaseproof paper. Using a rolling pin, roll over the paper until the mixture is 5mm thick, no more. Leave to set for 30 minutes.

4. Cut the set mixture into rectangles measuring about 10 x 7cm using a sharp knife, then cut the rectangles diagonally into triangles.

5. Heat a deep-fat fryer to 190°C, or heat the oil in a deep pan or a wok until very hot. To test the temperature, add a tiny piece of bread; it will sizzle when the oil is hot enough for frying.

6. Carefully lower the triangles into the hot oil, 5 or 6 at a time so they are not touching. Fry for about 4 minutes or until golden and crispy, moving them around. Remove with a slotted spoon and drain on kitchen paper. Repeat until you have fried all the triangles. Serve immediately.

SICILIAN-STYLE RICE CROQUETTES

Arancina bianca

This outstanding recipe came from Fabio Conticello, who owns the best focacceria in Palermo. If you can't find caciocavallo, use mozzarella. Alternatively, replace the cheese with a teaspoonful of cold ragù (Bolognese sauce) – a typical Sicilian addition.

Makes 8

½ teaspoon saffron threads

1.3 litres hot chicken or vegetable stock

6 tablespoons olive oil

1 large onion, peeled and finely chopped

400g Arborio or Carnaroli rice

150ml dry white wine

100g salted butter (room temperature)

50g freshly grated pecorino cheese

200g '00' grade pasta flour

100g caciocavallo cheese, rind removed and cut
 into 8 equal-sized pieces

150g fresh fine breadcrumbs

About 1 litre sunflower oil for deep-frying

Salt and freshly ground black pepper

1. First make the risotto. Put the saffron in a small bowl, add 4 tablespoons of the stock and set aside. Meanwhile, heat the olive oil in a large, heavy-based saucepan over a medium heat. Add the onion and fry gently, stirring, for 5 minutes. Add the rice and stir constantly for 3 minutes or until the grains are shiny.

2. Pour over the wine and simmer for 1 minute. When it has evaporated, stir in the saffron mixture. Now start adding the remaining stock, 2 ladleful at a time. Bring to a simmer and stir continuously until the liquid has been absorbed, then repeat the process with the remaining stock until the rice is cooked but still has a slight bite. This will take 18–20 minutes and you may not need all the stock.

3. Remove the pan from the heat and stir in the butter and pecorino for about 30 seconds. Season with salt and pepper, cover and leave to rest for 15 minutes. Meanwhile, make the batter: put the flour in a bowl. Add 300ml cold water gradually, whisking until smooth and very runny. Set aside.

4. When the risotto has cooled, tip it onto a clean work surface. Using dampened hands, press and squeeze the risotto for about 5 minutes until the mixture becomes denser and more compact. Shape the rice into 8 equal-sized balls.

5. Take one ball in the palm of your hand and flatten it slightly. Place a piece of caciocavallo in the centre, mould the rice around the filling to enclose and squeeze tightly to seal. To make the conical shape, flatten one end and make the other more pointed. Repeat for all the balls. Dip each formed cone in the batter and roll lightly in the breadcrumbs until evenly coated.

6. Heat a deep-fat fryer to 190°C, or heat the vegetable oil in a deep pan or a wok until very hot. To test the temperature, add a tiny piece of bread; it will sizzle when the oil is hot enough for frying. Fry the croquettes in batches for about 8 minutes or until golden brown and hot in the middle. Remove with a slotted spoon and drain on kitchen paper. Serve hot.

LENTIL SOUP WITH PANCETTA

Zuppa di lenticchie con pancetta

In Sicily lentils are considered good luck and a symbol of prosperity as they're thought to resemble tiny coins. They're often eaten at New Year, to bring wealth for the forthcoming year. Sicilians usually like to add pasta to their lentil soup, but I don't think this recipe needs it as it's already very hearty. A chunk of bread to dip, perhaps, and it really is a meal in itself.

Serves 6

3 tablespoons olive oil

100g smoked pancetta, diced

1 large onion, peeled and finely chopped

1 carrot, peeled and finely chopped

2 celery sticks, finely chopped

150ml dry white wine

1.5 litres hot vegetable stock

250g dried green lentils, rinsed and drained

3 fresh sage leaves

1 bay leaf

1 sprig of fresh rosemary

2 tablespoons tomato purée

Salt and freshly ground black pepper

1. Heat the oil in a large saucepan over a medium heat. Add the pancetta and fry for 3 minutes, stirring occasionally. Add the onion, carrot and celery and fry for 5 minutes or until softened.

2. Increase the heat and pour in the wine. Bring to the boil and let it bubble for 2 minutes. Add the stock and lentils and bring to the boil.

3. Make a bouquet garni by binding together the sage, bay leaf and rosemary using a little string. Drop it into the pan and stir in the tomato purée. Simmer for 30 minutes, stirring occasionally.

4. Remove and discard the bouquet garni and season with salt and pepper.

5. Remove 2 ladlesful of soup from the pan and put in a measuring jug. Using a hand-held blender, whizz the soup until it becomes smooth. Pour it back into the saucepan and stir. Serve hot.

CHESTNUT & FENNEL SOUP WITH SAGE

Zuppa di castagne e finocchi con salvia

Italy is the world's third largest producer of chestnuts and Sicilians love them. Ever since I moved to the UK, I've slowly started to associate chestnuts with Christmas, but I must revert to my former thinking – chestnuts can be, and should be, enjoyed all year round. This recipe uses frozen chestnuts so availability will not be an issue.

Serves 6

350g frozen chestnuts
70g salted butter
1 large onion, peeled and roughly chopped
1 leek (white only), roughly chopped
1 fennel bulb, cored and roughly chopped

8 fresh sage leaves, finely chopped
100ml dry white wine
1 litre hot chicken stock
50g mascarpone cheese
Salt and white pepper

1. Place the chestnuts in a small saucepan and pour over enough boiling water to cover. Place over a medium heat and simmer for 5 minutes. Drain and set aside. Reserve 3 chestnuts for the garnish.

2. Melt 50g of the butter in a large saucepan over a medium heat. Add the onion, leek, fennel and half the sage and fry for 10 minutes, stirring occasionally.

3. Increase the heat and pour in the wine. Bring to the boil and let it bubble for 2 minutes. Add the stock and chestnuts, bring to the boil then reduce the heat and simmer for 20 minutes, stirring occasionally.

4. Remove from the heat and blitz the soup using a blender or food processor. Add the mascarpone and blitz again until smooth, then season with salt and pepper. Return to a medium heat for 2 minutes. Meanwhile, finely chop the reserved chestnuts.

5. In a small frying pan melt the remaining butter. Fry the chopped chestnuts with the remaining sage and a pinch of salt for 3 minutes or until the sage is slightly crispy.

6. Ladle the soup into warm bowls and garnish with the chestnut and sage mixture.

PASTA, RISOTTO & PIZZA

Sicily

PASTA, RISOTTO & PIZZA

During Arab rule, Sicilians were introduced to the technique of drying pasta and they have never looked back. More often than not, dried pasta made from durum wheat is a preferred option to the richer, egg-based fresh pasta that is popular in northern Italy. Hard durum wheat gives the pasta a firmer texture, allowing the perfect al dente bite.

Seafood is the key component of many Sicilian recipes and pasta dishes are no exception. You can find so many options – tuna and anchovies are common in pasta sauces, as are prawns, squid, clams and mussels. Vegetables also feature highly in pasta sauces – usually in a tomato-based sauce and served with cheese. For vegetarians, I've included a recipe for Sicilian pesto – a punchy alternative to ordinary pesto – and an orzo pasta salad – another Sicilian delicacy – containing juicy orange segments and pistachios.

The risottos in Sicily tend to be simple and usually based on vegetables or seafood. Unlike in Sardinia, meat is not generally used.

Traditional Sicilian pizza has a thick crust and is often rectangular in shape rather than round. Additional flavourings are sometimes placed on top of the regular toppings of cheese and meat to prevent the dough from getting soggy. Each region has its own method of preparing pizza and it was hard to decide which to choose for this chapter as there were so many amazing options; for contrast, I have opted for a traditional, deep-pan version with anchovies, capers and olives, and a lighter one with a crispier base topped with courgettes and courgette flowers. Enjoy!

BUCATINI WITH SICILIAN PESTO

Bucatini al pesto siciliano

Classic pesto is a specialty of Liguria, in northwestern Italy. However, Sicilians have their own equally delicious, lesser-known version – just a few additional ingredients take it in an entirely new and exciting direction. In this recipe I've used bucatini pasta, which is basically a thicker version of spaghetti with a hole all the way through, but of course pasta of any shape will be fine.

Serves 4

350g fresh ripe tomatoes
75g blanched almonds
25g raisins
20g capers, drained
2 garlic cloves, peeled
2 fresh, medium-hot red chillies, deseeded
30g fresh basil leaves

20g fresh flat-leaf parsley
80ml extra virgin olive oil
Juice of ½ lemon
75g freshly grated Parmesan cheese, plus extra
 for sprinkling
500g dried bucatini
Salt

1. Blitz the tomatoes in a blender or food processor and tip into a sieve set over the sink to drain.

2. Return the tomatoes to the blender and add the almonds, raisins, capers, garlic, chillies, basil, parsley, oil and lemon juice. Blitz until smooth and pour into a medium bowl. Stir in the Parmesan and season with salt.

3. Meanwhile, cook the bucatini in a large pan of boiling, salted water until al dente. Reserve 80ml of the cooking water. Drain the pasta thoroughly and tip it back into the same pan with the cooking water.

4. Pour over the pesto and stir for 30 seconds to combine. Serve immediately with a little Parmesan sprinkled over the top.

FUSILLI WITH PANCETTA, PEAS & LEMON

Fusilli lunghi con pancetta, piselli e limone

The smoky flavour of the pancetta in this dish is perfectly offset by the bright notes of the lemon zest, while the peas add sweetness, colour and texture. Fusilli lunghi col buco always makes me smile – it's like long golden ringlets or spaghetti with a perm! I've chosen it for this dish as all the ingredients for the sauce get tangled up with the curls (and it reminds me of my daughter's hair). However, if you can't get hold of it use any long shape that you like.

Serves 4

6 tablespoons extra virgin olive oil

250g smoked pancetta, diced

3 large garlic cloves, peeled and thinly sliced

150g frozen peas, defrosted

½ teaspoon dried chilli flakes

5 tablespoons chopped fresh flat-leaf parsley

20 fresh yellow cherry tomatoes, quartered

500g dried fusilli lunghi col buco

Grated zest of 1 unwaxed lemon

100g freshly grated Parmesan cheese

Salt

1. Heat the oil in a large frying pan over a medium heat. Fry the pancetta for 4 minutes, stirring occasionally. Add the garlic, peas, chilli flakes and parsley, season with salt and fry for 3 minutes. Stir in the tomatoes and fry for 2 minutes.

2. Meanwhile, cook the fusilli in a large pan of boiling, salted water until al dente. Drain the pasta thoroughly and tip it back into the same pan.

3. Pour over the pancetta and pea mixture, add the lemon zest and stir for 30 seconds to combine. Sprinkle over the Parmesan and serve immediately.

ORZO PASTA SALAD WITH RED ONION, PISTACHIOS, CITRUS & FRESH HERBS

Insalata di orzo con agrumi, cipolle rosse e pistacchio

Orzo is a form of pasta shaped like a large grain of rice. It's perfect in a pasta salad but is equally at home in a casserole, soup or in stuffed vegetables such as peppers or tomatoes. This salad is ideal for picnics, buffets and packed lunches as it holds up well and can be made ahead. If you have any left over you can store it in the fridge in an airtight container for up to 48 hours.

Serves 4

1 vegetable stock cube

400g dried orzo pasta

2 oranges

1 large red onion, peeled and thinly sliced

Grated zest of 1 unwaxed lemon

10 fresh mint leaves, shredded

3 tablespoons chopped fresh flat-leaf parsley

30g pistachios, roughly chopped

200ml extra virgin olive oil

Balsamic glaze for drizzling

Salt and freshly ground black pepper

1. Put 4 litres of water in a large pan and bring to the boil, then crumble in the stock cube. Add the orzo and cook until al dente. Tip into a sieve set over the sink then rinse immediately under cold running water. Leave to drain for at least 5 minutes, shaking the colander every minute or so to make sure the pasta doesn't stick.

2. Meanwhile, peel and segment the oranges. Using a sharp knife, cut off about 1–2cm from the top and bottom of the fruit to expose the flesh. Place the fruit on one of its flat ends and cut down to remove the skin and the white pith. Rotate and repeat, working your way around the orange until the flesh is completely exposed.

3. Working over a large bowl to catch the juice, cut between the flesh and the white membrane to free the segments. Discard the membrane and put the segments into the bowl.

4. Add the onion, lemon zest, mint, parsley and pistachios to the bowl. Season well with salt and pepper. Add the cooked orzo and the oil. Gently fold everything together so the orzo is thoroughly coated in the mixture. Cover with cling film and set aside for about 15 minutes to allow the flavours to combine, stirring occasionally.

5. Stir once more and transfer to a large serving platter. Drizzle over some balsamic glaze. Serve at room temperature.

FETTUCCINE WITH TUNA & CAPER SAUCE

Fettuccine con salsa di tonno e capperi

Tuna live for much of the year in the Atlantic, but at the beginning of spring they start their exodus through the Mediterranean towards their warm-water spawning grounds off the coast of Sicily. Sicilians adore tuna and this dish is a storecupboard favourite in my house. It's best to use tuna chunks from a jar, although tinned tuna is fine too, provided it's in oil; avoid tuna in brine as it tastes like cat food! Please do not add any grated cheese to this dish, as it will ruin the flavour of the sauce.

Serves 4

6 tablespoons extra virgin olive oil
1 large red onion, peeled and thinly sliced
2 x 400g tins of chopped tomatoes
3 tablespoons chopped fresh flat-leaf parsley
100g capers, drained

1 teaspoon sugar
320g tuna chunks in oil (preferably in a jar), drained
500g fresh or dried fettuccine
Salt and freshly ground black pepper

1. Heat the oil in a large frying pan over a medium heat. Fry the onion for 8 minutes, stirring occasionally. Add the tomatoes, parsley, capers and sugar and season with salt and pepper. Bring to the boil.

2. Add the tuna, gently breaking up the larger chunks, and stir. Reduce the heat to low and simmer for 15 minutes, stirring occasionally.

3. Meanwhile, cook the fettuccine in a large pan of boiling, salted water until al dente. Drain the pasta thoroughly and tip it back into the same pan.

4. Pour over the tuna sauce and stir for 30 seconds to combine. Serve immediately.

CELERY & LEEK RISOTTO

Risotto al sedano e porri

Risottos are so creamy, luxurious and warming and they're also very versatile – you can adjust recipes according to what's in season and include meat, seafood or simply vegetables. This simple dish, containing celery, leeks and two types of cheese, makes a quick and inexpensive weekday meal – you can pick up the ingredients on your way home from work and you'll have a delicious meal on the table within 40 minutes.

Serves 4

450g celery sticks
100g salted butter
3 tablespoons extra virgin olive oil
2 leeks, about 300g in total, finely sliced
400g Arborio or Carnaroli rice

125ml dry white wine
1.5 litres hot vegetable stock
80g freshly grated Parmesan cheese
100g mascarpone cheese
Salt and white pepper

1. Dice the celery into 5mm pieces and finely slice the central leaves. Set aside.

2. Heat the butter and oil in a medium saucepan over a medium heat. Add the diced celery and leeks and fry gently for 8 minutes or until softened but not browned, stirring occasionally. Add the rice and stir constantly for 2 minutes or until the grains are coated and shiny.

3. Pour over the wine and simmer for about 1 minute until it has evaporated. Add 2 ladlesful of the stock, bring to a simmer and stir until it is absorbed.

4. Continue adding the stock in the same way, stirring and waiting for it to be absorbed before adding more, until the rice is cooked but still has a slight bite. It should take about 16–18 minutes. You may not need to add all the stock.

5. Remove the pan from the heat and add the Parmesan and mascarpone, stirring for about 30 seconds until creamy, then season with salt and pepper.

6. To serve, spoon the risotto onto warm plates and scatter over the celery leaves.

CREAMY LEMON RISOTTO WITH SEARED PRAWNS

Risotto cremoso al limone e gamberoni scottati

The delicate flavour of prawns pairs perfectly with a simple creamy lemon risotto and transforms it into something very elegant. Lemons are abundant in Sicily – they thrive in the volcanic soil and hot, sunny climate – and their flavour and aroma are outstanding, so they're used a lot in Sicilian dishes. When I was in Sicily filming for the TV series I spent a fabulous day visiting a citrus orchard and made this as a thank you for the wonderful people I met there (see page 245). If you want something extra special, try this dish with seared scallops instead of prawns.

Serves 4

4 tablespoons olive oil
2 shallots, peeled and finely chopped
375g Arborio or Carnaroli rice
300ml dry white wine
1 litre hot vegetable stock

Grated zest and juice of 2 unwaxed lemons
2 tablespoons chopped fresh flat-leaf parsley
60g mascarpone cheese
Salt and white pepper
16 raw, peeled king prawns, deveined

1. Heat half the oil in a medium saucepan over a medium heat. Add the shallots and fry gently for 5 minutes, stirring occasionally, until softened but not browned. Add the rice and stir constantly for 2 minutes or until the grains are coated and shiny.

2. Pour over the wine and simmer for about 1 minute until it has evaporated. Add 2 ladlesful of the stock, bring to a simmer and stir until it is absorbed.

3. Continue adding the stock in the same way, stirring and waiting for it to be absorbed before adding more, until the rice is cooked but still has a slight bite. It should take about 16–18 minutes. You may not need to add all the stock.

4. Remove the pan from the heat and add the lemon zest, three-quarters of the lemon juice, the parsley and mascarpone, stirring for about 30 seconds until creamy. Season with salt and pepper and keep warm while you cook the prawns.

5. Heat the remaining oil in a large frying pan over a high heat. Season the prawns with salt and pepper and fry for 2 minutes each side. Pour over the remaining lemon juice.

6. To serve, spoon the risotto onto warm plates and arrange 4 prawns on top of each portion, then drizzle over some of the oil and lemon juice that the prawns were cooked in.

PIZZA TOPPED WITH COURGETTE RIBBONS & FLOWERS

Pizza con nastri e fiori di zucchine

Sicilians are crazy about courgettes, particularly the flowers, which have a wonderful sweet, delicate flavour that goes beautifully with the saltiness of the pecorino on this pizza. If you grow your own vegetables you'll be familiar with them, but they can be tricky to find in the shops. However, they are available online and you may well know gardeners with a vegetable patch or allotment who could share them with you.

Makes 2

200g strong plain flour, plus extra for dusting
1 x 7g sachet fast-action (easy blend) dried yeast
¾ teaspoon salt
2 tablespoons extra virgin olive oil, plus extra for greasing

For the topping
2 x 125g balls of mozzarella, drained and sliced
2 tablespoons freshly grated pecorino cheese
4 baby courgettes
4–8 courgette flowers
Extra virgin olive oil for drizzling
16 small fresh basil leaves
Salt and freshly ground black pepper

1. Place the flour in a large bowl. Add the yeast to one side of the bowl and the salt to the other. Make a well in the centre and add the oil then gradually pour in 140ml warm water and mix together using the handle of a wooden spoon.

2. Knead the dough on a lightly floured surface for about 5 minutes or until soft, smooth and elastic, adding a little more flour if it's really sticky.

3. Shape the dough into a round and place in a large oiled bowl. Brush the top with a little oil and cover with cling film. Leave to rest at room temperature for 20 minutes. Brush 2 baking sheets with oil and set aside. Preheat the oven to 220°C/gas mark 7.

4. Turn out the dough onto a lightly floured surface and knead just 3 or 4 times to knock out the air.

5. Halve the dough and roll out each half directly onto an oiled baking sheet, rolling and stretching the dough to make 2 rounds about 25cm in diameter and 1–2cm thick. Make a small rim by pulling up the edges slightly.

6. To make the topping, scatter the mozzarella and pecorino evenly over the surface of the pizza bases, avoiding the rim. Using a vegetable peeler, shave the courgettes into long, thin strips, or ribbons, and arrange them on top of the pizzas. Remove the stamens from the courgette flowers and cut the flowers in half lengthways. Put on top of the cheeses. Season with salt and pepper and drizzle with oil.

7. Bake for 12–14 minutes or until golden brown. Remove from the oven, scatter over the basil and return to the oven for 1 further minute.

DEEP-PAN PIZZA WITH AN ANCHOVY, OLIVE & CAPER TOPPING

Pizza spessa con acciughe, olive e capperi

Sicily is the original home of the deep-pan pizza. A popular dish, it is usually cooked in large rectangular tins and sold by the weight. Pizzas in Sicily vary according to the region, with each area having its own recipes and traditions, and this type (known in Sicily as sfinciuni) originated in western Sicily, in the province of Palermo. I absolutely love the combination of anchovies, olives, capers and garlic in this topping.

Serves 10

500g strong white flour, plus extra for dusting
1 x 7g sachet fast-action (easy blend) dried yeast
2 teaspoons salt
6 tablespoons extra virgin olive oil, plus extra for greasing

For the topping
1 x 400g tin of chopped tomatoes
15 anchovy fillets in oil, drained
150g pitted green olives, drained and halved
1 tablespoon capers, drained
3 garlic cloves, peeled and thinly sliced
2 teaspoons dried oregano

1. Place the flour in a large bowl. Add the yeast to one side of the bowl and the salt to the other. Make a well in the centre and add 3 tablespoons of the oil then gradually pour in 300ml warm water and mix together using the handle of a wooden spoon.

2. Knead the dough on a lightly floured surface for about 10 minutes or until soft, smooth and elastic, adding a little more flour if it's really sticky.

3. Shape the dough into a round and place on a large oiled baking sheet. Brush the top with a little oil and cover with a clean tea towel. Leave to rise in a warm place for 1 hour or until nearly doubled in size.

4. Remove the tea towel. Using your fingertips, gently push the dough to a rectangle about 30 x 24cm and 2-3cm thick and make indentations in the dough. Brush with a little oil and replace the tea towel.

5. Leave to rise again in a warm place for a further 40 minutes or until nearly doubled in size. Meanwhile, preheat the oven to 220°C/gas mark 7.

6. Remove the tea towel and make further indentations in the dough. Spread over the chopped tomatoes, leaving a border of about 1cm clear around the edges. Scatter over the anchovies, olives, capers, garlic and oregano. Drizzle with the remaining oil.

7. Bake for 20-25 minutes or until golden brown. Transfer to a wire rack to cool slightly. Serve warm.

MAIN COURSES

Sicily

MAIN COURSES

Fish and other seafood dominate the menus in Sicily – more so than in Sardinia. Anchovies, sardines, red and grey mullet, tuna, swordfish, sea bass, squid, octopus, sea anemone, cuttlefish, clams and mussels are all caught in the seas around the island and are served in a multitude of ways – baked, stuffed, sautéed, deep-fried, boiled, raw and cooked in flavoursome stews with tomatoes and olives.

I was completely in my element in Sicily, and the first thing I did when I arrived back in London was go to my local fishmonger, order some clams, toss them in spaghetti with garlic and white wine and sit with my family reliving my trip to the amazing fish market in Catania – La Pescheria – a few steps away from the Piazza Duomo. The smell, colours and crazy, raucous sales patter all allow you to lose yourself in the fantastic buzzy atmosphere. I loved every minute. The exciting battle to get the freshest, biggest fish is the goal – haggling over the price is secondary.

Although less popular than fish, meat is also enjoyed in Sicily. While lamb, veal and goat are probably the most common meats on the island, beef and pork are also available. In fact, one of my favourite traditional dishes is polpettone siciliano – a meat roll made from minced beef and pork stuffed with ham and caciocavallo cheese and served with fresh tomato sauce. Sicilian cuisine uses the rolling technique for many different recipes; it allows lots of different flavours to be incorporated within one dish – a delicious idea that works for any kind of meat. Chicken is traditionally thought of as country food and poultry has always been raised and cooked at home, where it is enjoyed in various forms.

In this chapter I've included a real mixture of recipes to reflect the diversity of Sicilian cuisine – simple family meals, impressive options for entertaining, slow-cooked stews to make ahead and quick dishes for you to rustle up at the last minute. I am sure you will find much to tempt you.

ASPARAGUS & PEA FRITTATA

Frittata con asparagi e piselli

Foraging for wild asparagus in spring is a pastime for many Sicilians. More often than not the spears, which are thinner and have a more bitter flavour than the cultivated vegetable, are cooked in a frittata – an egg-based dish that is like a quiche without the pastry. Here I use asparagus tips with peas and fresh mint, which makes a really vibrant-looking dish perfect for brunch, lunch or a light supper. It's good cold too.

Serves 4

200g asparagus tips
200g frozen peas
5 tablespoons olive oil
10 fresh mint leaves, finely chopped

50g freshly grated Parmesan cheese
8 medium eggs, lightly beaten
Salt and freshly ground black pepper

1. Cook the asparagus in a medium saucepan of boiling, salted water for 1 minute. Add the peas and boil for 2 minutes. Drain the vegetables thoroughly. Cut the asparagus into bite-sized pieces.

2. Heat the oil in a 24cm heavy-based, non-stick frying pan over a medium heat. Add the asparagus and peas and fry for 1 minute, stirring. Add the mint and some salt and pepper and fry for a further 2 minutes. Preheat the grill to medium high.

3. Stir the Parmesan and seasoning into the beaten eggs and pour the mixture over the vegetables. Tilt the pan so the eggs cover the bottom of the pan evenly, reduce the heat slightly and cook for 6 minutes without stirring.

4. Remove the pan from the heat and place under the hot grill for about 6 minutes or until set and golden brown.

5. Remove from the grill and leave to rest in the pan for 5 minutes then transfer to a serving plate. Cut into wedges and serve warm.

SWEET PEPPERS STUFFED WITH COUSCOUS, COURGETTES & PINE NUTS

Peperoni ripieni di couscous, zucchine e pinoli

The idea of stuffing vegetables was introduced to Sicily by the Arabs, who ruled the island for over 250 years. Couscous is traditional for this Sicilian recipe, but you can use cooked rice if you prefer, as is often the case elsewhere in the Mediterranean. Flavoured with fresh mint, and with pine nuts adding textural contrast, this dish makes a lovely light, meat-free meal and looks spectacular. Serve with a side salad.

Serves 6

1 x 400g tin of chopped tomatoes

2 courgettes, coarsely grated

8 fresh mint leaves, finely chopped

60ml chilli oil

3 garlic cloves, peeled and finely chopped

1 teaspoon salt

500ml hot vegetable stock

250g couscous

3 large red peppers

3 large yellow peppers

50g pine nuts

1. Preheat the oven to 180°C/gas mark 4. Put the tomatoes, courgettes, mint, chilli oil, garlic and salt in a medium bowl. Stir to combine and set aside.

2. Bring the stock to a boil. Place the couscous in a large heatproof bowl and pour over 350ml of the stock. Cover with cling film and leave for 10 minutes or until all the stock is absorbed. Fluff up the grains with a fork.

3. Meanwhile, prepare the peppers by slicing off the top and removing all the seeds and white pith. Slice a tiny section off the bottom so that the peppers can stand upright. Place them in a large roasting tin.

4. Tip the tomato and courgette mixture into the bowl with the couscous. Add the pine nuts. Stir to combine. Carefully spoon the mixture into the peppers.

5. Pour the remaining stock around the peppers. Cover with foil and bake for 25 minutes, then remove the foil and bake for a further 20 minutes. Serve hot or warm with the juices from the tin poured over.

ROLLED AUBERGINES STUFFED WITH RAISINS, CAPERS & WALNUTS

Involtini di melanzane ripieni di uva passa, capperi e noci

Aubergines were introduced to the Mediterranean region by the Arabs in the Middle Ages and Sicilians use them a lot in their cooking. Stuffing sliced aubergines with cheese, breadcrumbs and other goodies is a particularly popular way of serving them. Feel free to be creative with your fillings – this recipe is not about precision. Choose the heaviest aubergines you can find and cut just before cooking to avoid discoloration. Serve with a green salad.

Serves 4

20g raisins

50ml Marsala wine

5 tablespoons olive oil

2 shallots, peeled and finely chopped

3 tablespoons chopped fresh flat-leaf parsley

15 walnut halves, finely chopped

Grated zest and juice of 1 unwaxed lemon

30g dried white breadcrumbs

30g capers, drained and chopped

20g freshly grated pecorino cheese

3 large, long aubergines

8 bay leaves

4 tablespoons extra virgin olive oil

Salt and freshly ground black pepper

1. Soak 4 wooden skewers, about 30cm long, in cold water for at least 30 minutes.

2. To make the stuffing mixture, put the raisins in a small bowl or cup, pour over the Marsala and leave to soak for 20 minutes, then drain. Heat the olive oil in a medium saucepan over a medium heat. Add the shallots and fry for 5 minutes or until softened, stirring occasionally. Stir in the parsley, season with salt and pepper and remove from the heat. Add the walnuts, lemon zest, breadcrumbs, capers, pecorino and drained raisins. Stir to combine and set aside.

3. Preheat the oven to 180°C/gas mark 4. Bring a large saucepan of salted water to the boil. Using a long, sharp knife cut each aubergine lengthways into slices about 1cm thick. Discard the first and last slice. Use the 12 widest slices.

4. Drop the aubergine slices into the boiling water, bring back to the boil and simmer for 4 minutes or until softened. Drain thoroughly then spread out on kitchen paper to dry.

5. Place the aubergine slices on a board and spread the stuffing mixture equally on all the slices. Roll up each slice and thread 3 aubergine rolls on each skewer. Thread a bay leaf on either end of the skewer.

6. Arrange the skewers on a large oiled baking sheet. Season with salt and pepper and brush over the lemon juice and extra virgin olive oil. Bake for 40 minutes. Serve immediately.

SALT COD STEW

Stufato di baccalà

Salt cod is cod that has been preserved by salting then drying. It is very popular in many European countries – from Scandinavia to the Mediterranean – but strangely not in Britain. I hope to convert you, as it has a delicious smoky taste. You can usually find salt cod in the world aisle of large supermarkets. Note that it has to be soaked for 48 hours before cooking to rehydrate it and remove excess salt, and never use salt when cooking with it. Enjoy with lots of crusty bread to mop up the delicious sauce.

Serves 4

500g salt cod
2 waxy maincrop potatoes (preferably Desirée), peeled
 and cut into 3cm chunks
4 tablespoons plain flour
6 tablespoons olive oil
1 large onion, peeled and finely chopped
1 leek, finely chopped
2 celery sticks, finely chopped

100ml dry white wine
300ml hot vegetable stock
1 x 400g tin of chopped tomatoes
50g pitted black olives, drained and roughly chopped
30g capers, drained
3 tablespoons snipped fresh chives
White pepper

1. To prepare the salt cod, rinse thoroughly under cold running water. Place in a large bowl, pour over cold water, cover with cling film and put in the fridge. Leave to soak for 48 hours, changing the water often.

2. Place the potatoes in a small saucepan and cover with cold unsalted water. Bring to the boil and cook for 3 minutes. Drain and set aside.

3. Remove and discard the skin from the fish, then rinse and pat dry with kitchen paper. Cut into 4 even-sized pieces. Put the flour on a large plate and coat the fish evenly in the flour. Shake off any excess.

4. Heat half the oil in a large saucepan over a high heat. Add the fish and fry for 2 minutes each side. Remove the fish from the pan and set aside.

5. Reduce the heat to medium and pour in the remaining oil. When hot, add the onion, leek and celery and fry for 8 minutes, stirring occasionally. Increase the heat to high, pour in the wine and cook for 2 minutes to allow the alcohol from the wine to evaporate.

6. Add the stock, par-boiled potatoes, tomatoes, olives, capers and chives and stir to combine. Bring to a simmer and reduce the heat to medium.

7. Return the fish to the pan, submerging it in the sauce. Season with pepper. Cover and cook gently for 20 minutes. Serve immediately in warm bowls.

SARDINES STUFFED WITH CHESTNUTS, RAISINS & CITRUS

Sardine ripiene di castagne, uva passa e agrumi

Fresh sardines are in a different class from the tinned variety and are relatively inexpensive. Large and plump, they are served throughout the year in Sicily as part of the antipasti table, but they can also be served as a light main course. You can substitute the sardines with fresh anchovies or small trout if you prefer. Some fishmongers will 'butterfly' the fish if you ask them so it's ready for stuffing.

Serves 4

16 fresh sardines, scaled, gutted, washed and
  heads removed
50g frozen chestnuts
3 tablespoons olive oil, plus extra for greasing
1 onion, peeled and finely chopped
80g fresh white breadcrumbs
1 unwaxed orange (grated zest of ½ orange and juice of
  whole fruit)

Juice of 1 lemon
30g raisins
2 tablespoons chopped fresh flat-leaf parsley
2 tablespoons extra virgin olive oil
16 bay leaves
Salt and freshly ground black pepper

1. First prepare the sardines for stuffing. Open out a fish and place it, skin-side up, on the work surface. Firmly press along the spine until the fish is lying completely flat. Turn the fish over and carefully pull away the spine, running your finger beneath it to loosen. When you reach the tail-end, cut off the spine using scissors and discard and scrape away any remaining small bones. Rinse the fish under cold running water and pat dry with kitchen paper. Repeat for all the sardines.

2. Preheat the oven to 190°C/gas mark 5. Place the chestnuts in a saucepan and pour over enough boiling water to cover. Place over a medium heat and simmer for 5 minutes, then drain. Chop finely and set aside.

3. Heat the olive oil in a medium saucepan over a medium heat. Add the onion and fry for 5 minutes.

4. Add the breadcrumbs and fry for 3 minutes. Stir frequently. Take the pan off the heat and add the orange zest, half the orange juice and half the lemon juice. Add the raisins, parsley and chestnuts. Season well with salt and pepper. Pour in half the extra virgin olive oil and stir to combine.

5. Lay the sardines flat on the work surface, skin-side down. Place a large teaspoonful of the breadcrumb mixture at the head-end of each sardine, then roll up to enclose. Oil a baking dish measuring about 20 x 15cm. Lay the sardines in 2 rows in the dish with the tails sticking up. Lay a bay leaf on each one.

6. Drizzle over the remaining orange and lemon juice and extra virgin olive oil and season with salt and pepper. Bake for 15–20 minutes. Leave to cool slightly before serving.

RED MULLET WITH SAFFRON, FENNEL & TOMATOES

Triglie con zafferano, finocchi e pomodori

Red mullet is arguably Sicily's most loved fish and with its light pink skin it is surely one of the best-looking fish around. It has a beautiful delicate flavour that goes perfectly with the fennel and saffron in this recipe. It is found in British waters, but you may need to order it from your fishmonger.

Serves 4

1 teaspoon saffron threads
4 tablespoons plain flour
4 whole red mullet, each about 200g, scaled, gilled, gutted and cleaned, fins and tail trimmed
6 tablespoons olive oil
1 large red onion, peeled and finely sliced
1 fennel bulb, cored and finely sliced

1 tablespoon chopped fresh thyme
1 tablespoon chopped fresh flat-leaf parsley
60ml dry white wine
1 x 400g tin of chopped tomatoes
Grated zest and juice of 1 unwaxed lemon
4 bay leaves
Salt and freshly ground black pepper

1. Put the saffron in a small bowl, add 4 tablespoons of warm water and set aside.

2. Place the flour on a large plate and season with salt and pepper. Coat the mullet on both sides with the seasoned flour, shaking off any excess.

3. Heat the oil in a large frying pan over a high heat. Add the fish in batches and fry for 2 minutes each side or until golden brown.

4. Reduce the heat to medium. Add the onion, fennel, thyme and parsley and fry for 2 minutes.

5. Increase the heat, pour in the wine and bring to the boil. Add the tomatoes, reserved saffron mixture, and lemon zest and juice. Season with salt and pepper and tuck in the bay leaves. Cover and cook gently for 10 minutes or until the fish is cooked through.

SWORDFISH STEW

Stufatino di pesce spada

Swordfish, one of the fastest fish in the ocean, is a firm, meaty fish with a texture rather like fresh tuna. It's perfect to use in a stew, as it keeps its shape well. If you can't find fresh swordfish fillets, you can use monkfish instead. This dish goes beautifully with Sweet and Sour Green Lentils (page 220).

Serves 4

4 tablespoons olive oil
1 onion, peeled and thinly sliced
1 large carrot, peeled and finely chopped
1 celery stick, finely chopped
16 fresh red cherry tomatoes, quartered
1 large courgette, sliced into rounds 1cm thick
50g pitted green olives, drained and halved

30g capers, drained
200ml dry white wine
100ml hot vegetable stock
2 tablespoons tomato purée
2 bay leaves
800g skinless swordfish fillet, cut into 3cm cubes
Salt and freshly ground black pepper

1. Heat the oil in a large frying pan with a lid or a sauté pan over a medium heat. Add the onion, carrot and celery and fry for 5 minutes or until softened, stirring occasionally.

2. Add the tomatoes, courgette, olives and capers and fry for about 3 minutes. Pour over the wine and stock. Stir in the tomato purée and bay leaves. Bring to the boil then reduce the heat and simmer for 5 minutes until thickened slightly. Season with salt and pepper.

3. Add the fish to the sauce. Cover the pan and simmer gently for about 8 minutes or until the fish is just cooked and the vegetables are tender.

TRAPANI-STYLE COUSCOUS WITH FISH, TOMATOES & ALMONDS

Couscous alla trapanese con pesce, pomodori e mandorle

There are literally dozens of recipes for this classic Sicilian couscous dish, most of which have the addition of seafood and chilli – but here I've let the sweet white fish do the talking. The town of Trapani is famous for couscous, and there is an annual couscous festival there in September. Ask your fishmonger for end cuts and bones to flavour the sauce.

Serves 4

6 tablespoons olive oil
2 onions, peeled and chopped
6 tablespoons chopped fresh flat-leaf parsley
2 x 400g tins of chopped tomatoes
1 teaspoon caster sugar
1 litre hot vegetable stock
2 bay leaves

250g large fish bones and tails
300g couscous
¼ teaspoon ground cinnamon
1kg mixed white fish fillets (e.g. halibut, haddock, cod, pollack, sea bass), cut into 5cm cubes
10g flaked almonds
Salt and white pepper

1. Heat the oil in a large saucepan over a medium heat. Add the onions and parsley and fry for 5 minutes, stirring occasionally. Tip in the tomatoes, add the sugar and season with salt and pepper. Bring to the boil, then reduce the heat, cover and simmer gently for 10 minutes. Remove the lid and simmer for a further 10 minutes. Pour over the hot stock.

2. Remove the pan from the heat and blitz with a hand-held blender. Add the bay leaves and drop in the fish bones and tails. Return to the heat and gently simmer, covered, for 30 minutes. Remove the fish bones and tails and discard.

3. Put the couscous in a medium saucepan. Measure 450ml of the prepared sauce and pour over the couscous. Stir in 100ml of boiling water and the cinnamon. Cover with a lid and place over a very low heat for 5 minutes.

4. Meanwhile, submerge the fish in the remaining prepared sauce. Cover and simmer over a low heat for 15 minutes.

5. Remove the couscous from the heat and leave to stand, still covered, for 10 minutes. Fluff up the couscous with a fork.

6. Lift the fish out of the pan and arrange on the couscous. Pour over some of the sauce and scatter over the remaining parsley and almonds. Put the remaining sauce in a jug and hand it round separately.

BAKED SEA BASS FILLETS WITH ANCHOVIES, LEMON & HERBS

Filetti di spigola al forno con acciughe, limoni ed erbette

Sea bass – the queen of the ocean – is beautifully sweet and tender and ideal for this dish, although any white fish will work well. The anchovies give it a wonderful depth of flavour. Please make sure that the sea bass for this recipe is very fresh, otherwise it will crumble and break as you bake it in the oven. Serve hot with Sweet Peppers Stuffed with Couscous (see page 174).

Serves 4

4 tablespoons olive oil, plus extra for greasing
12 anchovy fillets in oil, drained
8 sea bass fillets, each about 100g
8 sprigs fresh thyme

2 unwaxed lemons (1 thinly sliced and 1 freshly squeezed)
4 tablespoons chopped fresh flat-leaf parsley
30g dried white breadcrumbs
Salt and freshly ground black pepper

1. Preheat the oven to 190°C/gas mark 5. Heat the oil in a small saucepan over a low heat. Add the anchovies and mash with a fork. As soon as the anchovies have melted into the oil, remove from the heat. Tip into a small bowl and leave to cool.

2. Grease a baking dish measuring about 25 x 30cm. Lay 4 sea bass fillets, skin-side down, in the dish. Spread half the mashed anchovies over the fish. Place a sprig of thyme and a couple of lemon slices on top of each fillet and season with salt and pepper.

3. Place the remaining sea bass fillets on top, skin-side up. Spread over the remaining mashed anchovies. Place the remaining sprigs of thyme on the fish and season with salt and pepper. Sprinkle the parsley and breadcrumbs over the fish.

4. Bake for 18 minutes. Transfer the fish to a serving platter and pour over the lemon juice.

SICILIAN SEAFOOD SALAD

Insalata di mare alla siciliana

Seafood salad seemed to be on every menu in every restaurant when I travelled through Sicily – it really captures the taste of the sea and looks magnificent. I like to buy fresh whole squid for this recipe, but if you're short of time prepared squid tubes are available; however, they won't have the decorative tentacles attached.

Serves 6

400g live clams
450g live mussels
250g fresh whole squid
3 tablespoons olive oil
2 garlic cloves, peeled and finely sliced
350g raw, peeled king prawns, deveined
1 large red onion, peeled and thinly sliced
10 fresh red cherry tomatoes, halved
50g pitted green olives, drained and sliced
200g celery sticks (preferably young, tender stalks), thinly sliced

3 tablespoons chopped fresh flat-leaf parsley
Salt

For the dressing
1 fresh, medium-hot red chilli, finely chopped
Juice of 1 lemon
100ml extra virgin olive oil
30g capers, drained and chopped

1. Soak the clams in cold, salted water for 1 hour then drain well. Remove the 'beards' of the mussels by pulling the dark, stringy piece away from the shell. Scrub the mussels and clams under cold running water. Rinse away grit and remove barnacles with a small, sharp knife. Discard any open mussels or clams or those with broken shells. Set the shellfish aside.

2. To prepare the squid, pull the tentacles from the body. Feel inside the body and remove and discard the 'quill' (a transparent sliver of cartilage). Wash the inside of the body and peel off the outer skin. Cut the squid body into rings about 5mm wide and set aside.

3. Cut off the squid tentacles just below the eyes (discard the head and guts). Discard the small, hard 'beak' at the base of the tentacles. Rinse the tentacles in cold water and set aside.

4. Heat the olive oil in a large saucepan over a medium heat. Add the garlic, prawns, mussels, clams, and squid rings and tentacles. Cover and cook for 8 minutes or until the mussels and clams have opened, shaking the pan occasionally. Discard any mussels or clams that have not opened. Drain the seafood in a colander set over a bowl.

5. When cool enough to handle, remove the mussel and clam meat from the shells and put in a large bowl; discard the shells. Add the prawns and squid, then the onion, tomatoes, olives, celery and parsley. Stir well.

6. Place all the ingredients for the dressing in a small bowl and whisk to combine. Pour the dressing over the seafood. Mix everything together, season with salt and transfer to a large serving platter. Serve at room temperature.

SPICY SAUTÉED SQUID WITH MIXED OLIVES & CAPERS

Calamari piccanti saltati in padella con olive miste e capperi

Squid is one of the mainstays of the Sicilian diet and we saw it piled high in all the markets we visited in Sicily. Provided it's fresh and cooked properly it should be beautifully tender, not rubbery. The secret is to cook it either very slowly for a long time or very quickly over a high heat. Serve with crusty bread.

Serves 2

Pinch of saffron threads
4 tablespoons olive oil
350g fresh whole squid
2 tablespoons dry white wine
150ml hot fish stock
1 teaspoon dried chilli flakes

2 teaspoons tomato purée
30g capers, drained
50g pitted black olives, drained
50g pitted green olives, drained
2 tablespoons chopped fresh flat-leaf parsley
Salt and freshly ground black pepper

1. Put the saffron in a small bowl, add 4 tablespoons of warm water and set aside. Prepare the squid as described for Sicilian Seafood Salad (see page 187, steps 2 and 3). Cut the body into bite-sized pieces.

2. Heat the oil in a medium frying pan over a high heat. Add the squid and tentacles and fry for 1 minute, stirring occasionally. Drain and discard the excess liquid; keep the squid in the pan.

3. Return the pan to a high heat, add the wine and the saffron mixture and bring to the boil. Let it bubble for 1 minute, allowing the alcohol from the wine to evaporate.

4. Stir in the stock, chilli flakes, tomato purée, capers and olives. Season with salt and pepper. Bring to the boil and cook for 2 minutes. Transfer to a large serving bowl and scatter over the parsley. Serve immediately.

BAKED MUSSELS WITH ANCHOVIES & FRESH CHILLI

Cozze al forno con acciughe e peperoncino fresco

Mussels are so delicious and quick to cook. They are also relatively inexpensive and sustainable. This is a fantastic recipe that is very popular in Sicily and now just as popular in my house – it looks so impressive yet really isn't complicated to make. You can substitute the parsley with freshly chopped chives if you prefer. Serve with a bottle of chilled Sicilian white wine and lots of warm, crusty bread.

Serves 4

2kg live mussels

4 large garlic cloves, peeled

200ml dry white wine

4 tablespoons extra virgin olive oil

2 onions, peeled and finely chopped

2 fresh, medium-hot red chillies, deseeded and
  finely chopped

6 anchovy fillets in oil, drained

100g fresh white breadcrumbs

60g capers, drained

60g pitted green olives, roughly chopped

3 tablespoons chopped fresh flat-leaf parsley

Grated zest and juice of 1 unwaxed lemon

1. Preheat the oven to 220°C/gas mark 7. Scrub the mussels under cold running water. Rinse away grit and remove barnacles with a small, sharp knife. Remove the 'beards' by pulling the dark, stringy piece away from the mussel. Discard any open mussels or mussels with broken shells.

2. Place the mussels and garlic in a large saucepan and pour over the wine. Cover and cook over a high heat for about 5 minutes or until the mussels are open, shaking the pan occasionally. Tip into a colander placed over a bowl. Reserve 200ml of the cooking liquid and set aside. Discard the garlic and any mussels that remain closed.

3. Snap off and discard the empty shell from each mussel. Place the shells containing the mussels in a single layer, mussel-side up, in 2 large baking dishes or roasting tins. Set aside.

4. Heat the oil in a large frying pan over a medium heat. Add the onions and chillies and fry for 3 minutes, then stir in the anchovies and fry for 3 minutes. Finally, add the breadcrumbs, capers, olives and parsley and fry for 3 minutes.

5. Spoon the mixture over the mussels. Sprinkle over the lemon zest and juice. Drizzle over the reserved cooking liquid. Bake for 5 minutes or until the breadcrumbs are golden.

6. To serve, pile the baked mussels onto a large platter and serve immediately.

SPICY PRAWN, FENNEL, CHICKPEA & CAVOLO NERO BAKE

Gamberoni piccanti al forno con finocchi, ceci e cavolo nero

One of the great things about this recipe is that everything is contained in one dish. There is no need to make any accompaniment as it contains all the nutrition you need – simply serve it with a chunk of focaccia. Prawns and fennel are an amazing flavour combination, and the chickpeas add a buttery texture as well as making the dish more substantial. Cavolo nero has long been popular in Italy and is increasing in popularity in Britain, but if you can't find it in the shops use spinach instead.

Serves 6

3 tablespoons olive oil
1 fennel bulb, cored and thinly sliced
4 garlic cloves, peeled and crushed
½ teaspoon chilli powder
2 x 400g tins of chopped tomatoes
1 teaspoon chopped fresh oregano
1 teaspoon sugar

½ teaspoon salt
1 x 400g tin of chickpeas, rinsed and drained
100g cavolo nero, tough central midribs removed and
   leaves shredded
300g raw, peeled king prawns, deveined
2 x 125g balls of mozzarella, drained and roughly chopped

1. Preheat the oven to 190°C/gas mark 5. Heat the oil in a large frying pan over a medium heat. Add the fennel and fry for about 8 minutes, stirring occasionally, then add the garlic and chilli powder and fry for 1 minute.

2. Add the tomatoes, oregano, sugar and salt, bring to a simmer and cook gently for 8 minutes. Stir in the chickpeas, cavolo nero and prawns. Cook for 2 minutes.

3. Tip the contents of the frying pan into a baking dish measuring about 20 x 30cm.

4. Scatter mozzarella over the top and submerge some of it in the sauce. Bake for 20 minutes and serve immediately.

CHICKEN BREASTS IN MARSALA & TOMATO SAUCE WITH RAISINS

Petti di pollo con salsa al Marsala, pomodoro e uva passa

When I was filming for the TV series I visited Marco De Bartoli's vineyard in Samperi, near Marsala – an ancient town on the western edge of Sicily. I spent a wonderful day with his son, Renato De Bartoli, who told me about the history of Marsala wine – its production dates back to 1770, when an Englishman accidentally discovered the local fortified wine and shipped it to England, where it was soon in great demand. An industry grew in the region, and De Bartoli has been producing high-end wine for decades, using the native Grillo grape. As a thank you to the family, I cooked them this traditional Sicilian chicken dish using their wonderful wine. Serve with Garlic New Potatoes (pictured opposite and see page 226).

Serves 6

5 tablespoons plain flour
6 medium skinless, boneless chicken breasts
5 tablespoons olive oil
2 small onions, peeled and thinly sliced
250ml Marsala wine
700ml passata (sieved tomatoes)

1 teaspoon caster sugar
Grated zest of 1 unwaxed orange
75g raisins
10 fresh basil leaves
Salt and freshly ground black pepper

1. Put the flour on a large plate and season with salt and pepper. Dip the chicken breasts in the seasoned flour to coat.

2. Heat the oil in a large frying pan over a high heat. Add the chicken and fry for 2 minutes each side or until lightly browned. Remove the chicken from the pan and set aside.

3. Reduce the heat to medium. Add the onions and fry for 5 minutes or until softened, stirring occasionally. Increase the heat and pour in the Marsala. Bring to the boil and let it bubble for 2 minutes.

4. Stir in the passata, sugar, orange zest, raisins and basil. Season with salt and pepper. Reduce the heat to medium-low, return the chicken to the pan and cook gently for 20 minutes. Check for seasoning and serve immediately.

CHICKEN STEW WITH ARTICHOKES, TOMATOES & WHITE WINE

Stufato di pollo con carciofi, pomodori e vino bianco

The residents of Cerda, a town near Palermo, are such fans of artichokes that they've erected a giant statue of the vegetable in the main piazza. Each year in April they host the *Sagra del Carciofo*, a festival to mark the end of the artichoke season; restaurants present this elegant ingredient in every form possible, all of which are utterly delicious. Chicken goes beautifully with artichokes, and this recipe is in honour of the residents of Cerda. Serve with mash and Carrots Cooked in Marsala (see page 219).

Serves 6

12 boneless, skin-on chicken thighs, about 1kg in total
6 tablespoons olive oil
1 large red onion, peeled and finely chopped
4 tablespoons plain flour
200ml dry white wine
2 x 400g tins of chopped tomatoes

10 fresh basil leaves, plus extra to garnish
300ml hot chicken stock
280g chargrilled artichoke hearts in oil,
  drained and quartered
Salt and freshly ground black pepper

1. Season the chicken with salt and pepper. Heat the oil in a large flameproof casserole over a medium to high heat. When very hot, add half the chicken, skin-side down, and fry for about 5 minutes each side or until golden brown all over. Transfer to a large plate using a slotted spoon and set aside. Repeat for the remaining chicken.

2. Reduce the heat to medium. Add the onion and fry for 8 minutes or until softened, stirring and scraping the bottom of the casserole to release any sticky bits left from the chicken.

3. Return the chicken and its juices to the casserole. Sprinkle over the flour and fry for a further 2 minutes. Increase the heat to high and pour in the wine. Bring to the boil and let it bubble for 2 minutes.

4. Add the tomatoes and basil, season with salt and pepper and cook for 5 minutes.

5. Pour over the stock, reduce the heat to low, cover and simmer very gently for 30 minutes or until the chicken is cooked through and the sauce is thickened, turning the chicken at least 3 times.

6. Add the artichokes and bring to the boil. Reduce the heat, cover and simmer for 5 minutes. Transfer to warm bowls or plates and garnish with fresh basil.

CHICKEN BREASTS WITH WHITE WINE, SAFFRON & MASCARPONE SAUCE

Petti di pollo con salsa al vino bianco, zafferano e mascarpone

The beauty of chicken breasts lies in their versatility and simplicity – subtle and understated, they allow other ingredients to come to the fore. Here they're baked and served with a delicate-tasting, creamy saffron sauce. The beautiful colour reminds me of an old Sicilian proverb, 'Gold Attracts a Crowd' – and you will certainly attract a crowd whenever you serve this dish. If you don't have mascarpone cheese, you can use thick double cream instead. Serve with plain rice and a green vegetable.

Serves 6

2 pinches of saffron threads
5 tablespoons olive oil, plus extra for greasing
6 medium skinless, boneless chicken breasts
3 shallots, peeled and thinly sliced
150ml dry white wine

400ml hot chicken stock
Juice of 1 lemon
250g mascarpone cheese
2 tablespoons chopped fresh flat-leaf parsley
Salt and white pepper

1. Put the saffron in a small bowl, add 4 tablespoons of warm water and set aside. Preheat the oven to 180°C/gas mark 4. Grease a large baking sheet with oil.

2. Heat the olive oil in a large frying pan over a high heat. Season the chicken with salt and pepper and fry for 2 minutes each side or until golden. Transfer the chicken to the baking sheet and bake for 15 minutes.

3. Meanwhile, put the frying pan back on the hob and reduce the heat to medium. Add the shallots and fry for 2 minutes, stirring occasionally. Increase the heat and pour in the wine. Bring to the boil and let it bubble for about 3 minutes.

4. Pour in the chicken stock and stir in the saffron mixture. Bring to the boil, then reduce the heat and simmer gently for 10 minutes.

5. Stir in the lemon juice and mascarpone. Season with salt and pepper, add the parsley and cook for a further 3 minutes.

6. Remove the chicken from the oven and transfer to a serving platter. Spoon over the sauce.

SLOW-COOKED PORK RIBS IN TOMATO SAUCE WITH CANNELLINI BEANS

Stufato di costatelle di maiale al pomodoro e cannellini

I love a one-pot meal – minimum fuss, fewer dishes to juggle and less washing up! In this recipe the ribs are simmered slowly in a tomato sauce, and the result is beautifully tender meat that falls off the bone. The beans have a lovely creamy texture and make the dish that much more wholesome and substantial. Serve with some country-style bread to mop up the delicious sauce.

Serves 4

2 pinches of saffron threads
400ml hot vegetable stock
5 tablespoons olive oil
1kg pork spare ribs
1 large red onion, peeled and finely sliced

1 tablespoon chopped fresh rosemary
300ml passata (sieved tomatoes)
3 bay leaves
1 x 400g tin of cannellini beans, rinsed and drained
Salt and freshly ground black pepper

1. Put the saffron in a small bowl, add 4 tablespoons of the stock and set aside.

2. Heat the oil in a large saucepan over a high heat. When very hot, fry the ribs for about 3 minutes each side or until browned on all sides. You will need to do this in batches. Remove the ribs with a slotted spoon and transfer to a large plate.

3. Reduce the heat to medium, add the onion and rosemary and fry for 5 minutes, stirring occasionally. Return the ribs to the pan. Add the remaining stock, saffron mixture, passata and bay leaves and bring to the boil. Reduce the heat, cover and cook for 45 minutes, stirring occasionally.

4. Stir in the beans, cover again and cook for 20 minutes. Remove the lid and cook for a further 5 minutes to allow the sauce to thicken slightly. Season with salt and pepper. Serve immediately.

STUFFED SICILIAN MEAT ROLL

Polpettone siciliano

This is the Sicilian answer to meatloaf and it's one of my favourite comfort foods. Every household has its own version and there is a lot of flexibility when it comes to ingredients. Here I've used caciocavallo – a firm curd cheese with a slightly salty flavour – but Asiago or mozzarella are good too. If you like a bit of a kick, add a chopped fresh red chilli to the meat mixture – feel free to experiment.

Serves 6

3 tablespoons extra virgin olive oil
1 red onion, peeled and finely chopped
1 red pepper, deseeded and finely chopped
400g minced beef
400g minced pork
50g fresh white breadcrumbs
50g freshly grated Parmesan cheese
2 tablespoons tomato purée
2 large eggs, beaten
3 tablespoons chopped fresh flat-leaf parsley

100g sliced Italian cooked ham
150g caciocavallo cheese, cut into cubes
Salt and freshly ground black pepper

For the sauce
3 tablespoons extra virgin olive oil
1 red onion, peeled and finely chopped
2 x 400g tins of chopped tomatoes
6 fresh basil leaves

1. Preheat the oven to 180°C/gas mark 4. Heat the oil in a medium saucepan over a medium heat. Add the onion and red pepper and fry for 6 minutes or until softened, stirring occasionally. Set aside.

2. Put the beef and pork in a large bowl and add the breadcrumbs, Parmesan, tomato purée, eggs and parsley. Season with salt and pepper. Add the onion and pepper mixture. Mix well with your hands until everything is thoroughly combined.

3. Turn out the mixture onto a large sheet of baking parchment. Using your hands, flatten and shape the meat mixture to a rectangle measuring about 35 x 25cm. Arrange the ham slices on the top of the meat rectangle, leaving a small border of about 1cm all round. Scatter over the caciocavallo, again leaving a border around the edge.

4. Starting from one of the long edges, tightly roll up the meat like a Swiss roll (use the parchment to help by gently pulling it up and over as you roll). After rolling, ensure the join is underneath then transfer to a large oiled baking sheet. Bake for 1¼ hours.

5. Meanwhile, to make the sauce heat the oil in a medium saucepan over a medium heat. Add the onion and fry for 6 minutes or until softened, stirring occasionally. Add the tomatoes and basil and season with salt and pepper. Cook for 15 minutes, stirring occasionally. Take the pan off the heat and blitz with a hand-held blender until smooth. Keep warm.

6. Remove the meat roll from the oven and leave to rest for 10 minutes. Slice thickly and serve with the tomato sauce.

HERBY VEAL MEATBALLS WITH PARMESAN & PINE NUTS IN TOMATO SAUCE

Polpettine di vitello alle erbe con parmigiano e pinoli in salsa di pomodoro

Any fans of Mafia movies will be aware of the immense popularity of meatballs in Sicily, for instance in the memorable scene in *The Godfather* where 'Fat Pete' Clemenza shows young Michael Corleone the 'proper' way to cook them. When I was touring Sicily for the TV series I visited Bar Vitelli, where *The Godfather* was filmed. I chatted to Dario (the owner's son) about the making of the movie and then cooked him my own version of meatballs, which I'm sharing with you here. As *vitello* is Italian for veal, I felt veal meatballs were most fitting for the occasion. Rice with Cranberries, Lemon and Parsley (pictured opposite and see page 221) makes a great accompaniment.

Serves 6

1kg minced veal
150g fresh white breadcrumbs
100g freshly grated Parmesan cheese
50g pine nuts, chopped
2 tablespoons chopped fresh flat-leaf parsley
1 large egg, beaten
Juice and grated zest of 1 unwaxed lemon

4 tablespoons olive oil
180ml dry white wine
2 tablespoons tomato purée
500ml hot beef stock
4 bay leaves
Salt and freshly ground black pepper

1. Place the veal, breadcrumbs, Parmesan, pine nuts, parsley, egg and lemon zest and juice in a large bowl. Season with salt and pepper. Mix well with your hands until everything is thoroughly combined.

2. Using dampened hands, take small amounts of the veal mixture and roll into 5cm balls (about the size of a golf ball). It should make about 30 meatballs.

3. Heat the oil in a large flameproof casserole over a high heat. Add the meatballs and fry for about 5 minutes or until browned on all sides, turning carefully. You may need to do this in batches. Remove and drain on kitchen paper.

4. Increase the heat to high and pour the wine into the casserole. Bring to the boil and let it bubble for 2 minutes, scraping up any crispy bits from the bottom of the pan.

5. Stir in the tomato purée and return the browned meatballs to the casserole. Add the stock and bay leaves and bring to a simmer. Cover and simmer for a further 15 minutes. Serve immediately.

POT-ROASTED VEAL

Arrosto di vitello in casseruola

Italians love veal, and this is a wonderful roast dinner Sicilian style. Veal is generally considered a special occasion meat, but if you prefer this recipe can be made with a cheaper cut of beef, such as silverside or brisket, and cooked for a little longer to make sure the meat is really tender. The secret of success is in the long, slow cooking of the joint that makes it meltingly soft and delicious.

Serves 4

1kg piece of rose veal shoulder, rolled and tied
5 tablespoons olive oil
2 large onions, peeled and thinly sliced
2 large carrots, peeled and sliced into rounds 1cm thick
2 celery sticks, roughly chopped
100ml dry white wine

1 x 400g tin of chopped tomatoes
4 sprigs of fresh rosemary
1 teaspoon caster sugar
500ml hot beef stock
Salt and freshly ground black pepper

1. Preheat the oven to 180°C/gas mark 4. Season the veal with salt and pepper.

2. Heat the oil in a large flameproof casserole over a high heat. When very hot, add the veal and brown on all sides (it should take about 6 minutes). Remove the meat from the pan and set aside.

3. Reduce the heat to medium. Add the onions, carrots and celery and fry for 5 minutes, stirring occasionally and scraping up any crispy bits from the bottom of the pan.

4. Increase the heat to high and pour in the wine. Bring to the boil and let it bubble for 2 minutes. Add the tomatoes, rosemary and sugar. Season with salt and pepper. Bring to a simmer.

5. Return the veal to the pan. Pour over the stock and bring to a simmer. Transfer to the oven for 2 hours, turning the meat and stirring every 30 minutes.

6. Transfer the meat to a plate or board. Cover with foil and leave to rest for about 10 minutes.

7. Meanwhile, remove the rosemary sprigs from the casserole and discard. Using a hand-held blender, blitz the sauce until smooth. Carve the meat and serve with the sauce.

LAMB CUTLETS WITH A HERBY PISTACHIO & ORANGE CRUST

Costolette di agnello in crosta alle erbe, pistacchi ed arance

Lamb cutlets are often made with a herb crust, but the difference here is the pistachios – a Sicilian twist. The nuts give added crunch and their rich flavour really complements that of the sweet lamb. The crust not only adds flavour but it helps to keep the meat beautifully succulent and juicy. Serve with Green Bean, Spinach and Artichoke Salad (see page 216).

Serves 4

100g shelled pistachios
40g fresh white breadcrumbs
Grated zest of 1 unwaxed orange
¼ teaspoon dried chilli flakes

2 tablespoons chopped fresh flat-leaf parsley
½ teaspoon salt, plus extra for seasoning
6 tablespoons olive oil
12 lamb cutlets, about 2cm thick, trimmed

1. Preheat the grill to its highest setting. Grind the pistachios in a food processor or pestle and mortar (not too finely) and tip into a medium bowl.

2. Add the breadcrumbs, orange zest, chilli flakes, parsley and salt. Stir to combine then stir in half the oil. Set aside.

3. Brush both sides of the cutlets with the remaining oil and season with salt.

4. Grill the cutlets for 3 minutes each side, then remove from the grill and top one side with the pistachio mixture, pressing down firmly.

5. Return the cutlets to the grill for 1 minute. Watch the cutlets as they cook to ensure the crust does not burn. Serve immediately.

ROAST SHOULDER OF LAMB WITH GARLIC, ROSEMARY & PANCETTA

Spalla d'agnello arrosto con aglio, rosmarino e pancetta

Slow cooking really takes the stress out of serving a roast – you can put the joint in the oven and forget all about it until you're ready to eat, leaving you time to prepare other dishes, go for a walk, or sit on the sofa and relax. This slow-roasted shoulder of lamb is melt-in-the-mouth tender with the meat almost falling off the bone.

Serves 4

1 small shoulder lamb, about 1.7kg, trimmed
5 garlic cloves, peeled and quartered lengthways
20 small sprigs of fresh rosemary, about 1–2cm long
22 slices smoked pancetta or smoked streaky bacon
3 tablespoons extra virgin olive oil, plus extra for drizzling

500ml hot lamb or beef stock
5 bay leaves
3 tablespoons runny honey
2 unwaxed lemons, quartered lengthways
Salt and freshly ground black pepper

1. Preheat the oven to 160°C/gas mark 3. Make about 20 incisions in the top of the lamb (the side with the skin) with a sharp knife. Space these slits at regular intervals and make them about 2cm long and as deep as you can go. Insert a slice of garlic and a rosemary sprig into each slit.

2. Lay the pancetta or bacon slices over the top of the lamb, overlapping them slightly, and tuck in the ends underneath. Gently rub the oil over the pancetta and the underside of the lamb. Season the top with salt and pepper.

3. Place the lamb on a rack in a large roasting tin. Pour the stock into the tin and add the bay leaves. Cover the lamb tightly with a double layer of foil. Roast the lamb for 2 hours, checking after about 1½ hours as you may need to top up with a little more stock.

4. Remove the lamb from the oven and loosen the foil slightly, so the steam can escape. Set aside for 15 minutes. Meanwhile, increase the oven temperature to 220°C/gas mark 7.

5. Take the foil off the lamb and drizzle over the honey. Return the meat to the oven for 8 minutes or until the pancetta is golden and crispy.

6. Place the lamb on a large warm serving plate and slice or pull the meat – it should be very tender and come away from the bone easily. Drizzle over some of the oil and the roasting juices. Serve with the lemon quarters for squeezing over.

SIDE DISHES

Sicily

SIDE DISHES

Sicily is sometimes referred to as 'God's kitchen', and it's easy to see why – the island produces such an amazing variety of fruit and vegetables. They are harvested in their prime and sold in season, allowing you to appreciate their fantastic taste to the full.

One of the great joys of being in Sicily is visiting the bustling markets and shopping for the finest-quality seasonal vegetables. In spring you'll find fabulous artichokes, asparagus and fresh garlic; in summer aubergines, peppers, courgettes and tomatoes; in autumn wild mushrooms and olives; and from winter to early spring purple cauliflower and broccoli. Remember, although you can buy almost any vegetable at any time of year in Britain, for best results in cooking it is always best to use vegetables when they're in season – it really does make a difference not only to flavour but also colour and texture.

While the quality of ingredients is really important, I also think one of the great skills of cooking is choosing side dishes that are the perfect match for the main dish. For instance, if you're serving plain grilled fish or meat you'll want a full-flavoured accompaniment; conversely, if you're serving a rich main you'll be better off with simpler, cleaner flavours. Look at the meal as a whole and provide a balance of flavours and textures without repetition. Remember, you can serve many of the vegetable-based dishes featured in the Antipasti & Soups and Main Courses chapters as side dishes – so feel free to get creative with your menus.

GREEN BEAN, SPINACH & ARTICHOKE SALAD WITH SAFFRON DRESSING

Insalatona siciliana di fagiolini, spinaci e carciofi con condimento allo zafferano

Beans, spinach and artichoke hearts are a wonderful combination, but it is the saffron dressing that really makes this salad sing. One of the world's most expensive spices, saffron comes from the dried stigmas of the saffron crocus – the stigmas can be picked only by hand and 250,000 of them are required to make just half a kilo of saffron. It adds a beautiful earthy flavour as well as a golden colour redolent of Sicilian sunshine. This salad can also be served as a first course.

Serves 6

200g fine green beans, trimmed

30g raisins

180g chargrilled artichoke hearts in oil, drained and
  quartered

50g walnut halves, broken into pieces

2 tablespoons olive oil

4 shallots, peeled and finely sliced

½ teaspoon dried chilli flakes

100g baby spinach leaves

Salt

For the dressing

Grated zest and juice of 1 unwaxed lemon

1 tablespoon white wine vinegar

Large pinch of saffron threads

1 tablespoon runny honey

6 tablespoons extra virgin olive oil

1. Bring a small saucepan of salted water to the boil and cook the beans for 3–4 minutes or until just tender. Drain and rinse under cold running water (so they retain their crunch), then drain again thoroughly. Cut into 2cm lengths. Set aside.

2. Place the raisins in a small bowl or cup, cover with boiling water and leave to soak for 20 minutes; drain.

3. To make the dressing, place the lemon zest and juice, vinegar and saffron in a small saucepan. Heat very gently for about 1 minute or until the saffron threads start to dissolve. Remove from the heat and stir in the honey and oil. Set aside to cool completely.

4. Place the green beans, artichoke hearts and walnuts in a large bowl and pour over the dressing. Scatter over the raisins and season with salt. Toss together to combine.

5. Heat the oil in a small saucepan over a medium heat. Add the shallots and gently fry for 5 minutes until very soft, stirring occasionally. Add the chilli flakes and fry for 2 minutes. Remove from the heat and leave to cool slightly.

6. Arrange the spinach on a large serving platter. Spoon the artichoke heart and bean mixture over the spinach and top with the shallot mixture.

CARROTS COOKED IN MARSALA

Carote cotte al Marsala

Marsala wine – a Sicilian delicacy – transforms the humble carrot into something really elegant in this popular dish, imparting a rich caramel flavour. If you don't have Marsala, you can use sweet sherry instead. Please do not overcook the carrots – they should be al dente. Good to accompany any meat dish.

Serves 4

4 tablespoons olive oil
2 large garlic cloves, peeled
500g carrots, peeled and cut into rounds 5mm thick
1 teaspoon caster sugar
¼ teaspoon salt

2 bay leaves
¼ teaspoon dried chilli flakes
150ml Marsala wine
2 tablespoons chopped fresh flat-leaf parsley

1. Heat the oil in a medium saucepan over a medium heat. 'Bruise' the garlic by placing the peeled cloves on a board, setting the flat side of a knife on top and pressing down with your palm to flatten slightly. Add the garlic to the hot oil and fry for 5 minutes, then discard.

2. Add the carrots, sugar, salt, bay leaves and chilli flakes to the pan and fry for 2 minutes.

3. Pour in the Marsala and cook, stirring occasionally, for a further 12 minutes or until the carrots are cooked but al dente. Stir in the parsley and serve immediately.

SWEET & SOUR GREEN LENTILS WITH TOMATOES, FRESH HERBS & CHILLI

Lenticchie in agrodolce con pomodori, erbette e peperoncino

This is one of my favourite lentil side dishes. It's sweet, sour and spicy all in one delicious mouthful and is also extremely versatile – great for vegetarians and also as an accompaniment with fish or meat, particularly pork sausages. Sometimes I put it on toasted ciabatta bread for a wholesome lunchtime treat. *Fantastico*!

Serves 4

4 tablespoons olive oil
1 red onion, peeled and thinly sliced
1 tablespoon chopped fresh oregano
1 tablespoon chopped fresh rosemary
1 x 400g tin of green lentils, rinsed and drained

1 x 400g tin of chopped tomatoes
3 tablespoons red wine vinegar
¼ teaspoon chilli powder
1 teaspoon caster sugar
½ teaspoon salt

1. Heat the oil in a medium saucepan over a medium heat. Add the onion and fry for 5 minutes, stirring occasionally. Add the oregano and rosemary and fry for 1 minute.

2. Tip in the lentils and tomatoes. Add the vinegar, chilli powder, sugar and salt. Bring to the boil, cover and simmer gently for 10 minutes. Serve hot or at room temperature.

RICE WITH CRANBERRIES, LEMON & PARSLEY

Riso con mirtilli rossi, limone e prezzemolo

Long before rice was known on mainland Italy it was a key crop in Sicily because the Arabs introduced it in the Middle Ages. Another Arab-influenced element of Sicilian cuisine is the popular addition of dried fruits to dishes to add sweetness and texture. Here I decided to jazz up bland rice with softened dried cranberries, lemon and fresh parsley. It's such a simple way to give a dish a new twist and you can use any dried fruits you have in your cupboard. It goes perfectly with Herby Veal Meatballs (see page 204 and pictured on page 205).

Serves 4

50g dried cranberries
4 tablespoons dry white wine
350g long-grain rice
Grated zest and juice of 1 lemon

2 tablespoons olive oil
2 tablespoons chopped fresh flat-leaf parsley
Salt and freshly ground black pepper

1. Put the cranberries in a small bowl and spoon over the wine. Leave to soak.

2. Rinse the rice thoroughly under cold water until the water runs clear and drain. Tip into a saucepan with a tight-fitting lid. Add 700ml cold water and a good pinch of salt.

3. Bring to the boil. Stir, reduce the heat to low and cover. Simmer gently for 8 minutes or until all the water has been absorbed. Remove from the heat, but keep the lid on. Leave to stand for 10 minutes. Fluff up the grains with a fork.

4. Put the rice in a large bowl. Add the cranberries, lemon zest and juice, oil and parsley. Season with some salt and pepper and gently mix all the ingredients together.

SPICY SPINACH, MUSHROOMS, GREEN BEANS & COURGETTE WITH PARMESAN

Spinaci piccanti con funghi, fagiolini, zucchine e parmigiano

Bursting with flavour, this vegetable side dish is likely to convert even the most red-blooded of carnivores. It is also highly nutritious – spinach is full of vitamins and iron, mushrooms are also a good source of iron as well as selenium and vitamin B, and courgettes are high in antioxidants and promote all-round cardiovascular health. On top of that, Parmesan is one of the healthiest cheeses, being packed with protein and calcium and high in vitamin A. It is also lactose free, so suitable for those who are lactose-intolerant. In short, this is a superfood side dish!

Serves 6

5 tablespoons extra virgin olive oil
1 large red onion, peeled and thinly sliced
100g chestnut mushrooms, quartered
250g fine green beans, cut into 2cm lengths
1 courgette, cut into rounds 5mm thick
50ml dry white wine

½ teaspoon dried chilli flakes
250g baby spinach leaves
Juice of ½ orange
40g freshly grated Parmesan cheese
Salt and freshly ground black pepper

1. Heat the oil in a large saucepan over a medium heat. Add the onion and fry for 5 minutes or until softened, stirring occasionally. Add the mushrooms, beans and courgette. Season well with salt and pepper. Fry for 5 minutes, stirring frequently.

2. Increase the heat to high and pour in the wine. Bring to the boil and let it bubble for 1 minute. Reduce the heat and add the chilli flakes and spinach and cook for 5 minutes or until the spinach wilts.

3. Pour over the orange juice. Sprinkle over the Parmesan, check for seasoning and stir to combine. Serve immediately.

SPICY CAULIFLOWER WITH MUSHROOMS, OLIVES, RAISINS & PINE NUTS

Cavolfiore piccante con funghi, olive, uva passa e pinoli

Sicilian cauliflowers are usually a bright pea-green colour and occasionally dark purple. However, for this recipe I've used the traditional British white variety and it works beautifully. This dish is earthy and satisfying, and it's tasty either as an accompaniment to grilled meat or served on its own as a lunch dish. Alternatively, stir it through some hot pasta and top with grated Parmesan cheese.

Serves 6

1 large cauliflower, about 600g, cut into bite-sized florets
250g chestnut mushrooms, quartered
4 bay leaves
5 tablespoons chilli oil
100g pitted black olives, drained and halved
30g dried breadcrumbs

50g raisins
30g toasted pine nuts
Juice of ½ lemon
1 tablespoon chopped fresh oregano
Salt

1. Preheat the oven to 180°C/gas mark 4. Bring a pan of salted water to the boil, add the cauliflower florets and simmer for 1 minute, then drain.

2. Place the parboiled cauliflower in a baking dish measuring about 25 x 30cm. Add the mushrooms and bay leaves. Drizzle with the chilli oil, season with salt and toss together so the vegetables are well coated in the oil. Scatter over the olives and breadcrumbs. Roast for 20–30 minutes or until golden brown and the cauliflower is tender.

3. Meanwhile, place the raisins in a small bowl or cup, cover with boiling water and leave to soak for 20 minutes, then drain.

4. Tip the roasted vegetables onto a large serving platter. Scatter over the raisins and pine nuts, sprinkle over the lemon juice and garnish with the oregano. Serve immediately.

GARLIC NEW POTATOES WITH A PARMESAN CRUST

Patate novelle all'aglio gratinate con parmigiano

New potatoes have a waxy texture and keep their shape once cooked so are perfect for this recipe. I sometimes find that plain new potatoes can be a bit dull, but this recipe with garlic and a crisp Parmesan topping takes them to a higher level. Good to accompany any meat or vegetarian main course.

Serves 4

16 baby new potatoes, scrubbed
50g salted butter
1 large garlic clove, peeled and crushed
1 teaspoon chopped fresh thyme

1 teaspoon chopped fresh rosemary
30g freshly grated Parmesan cheese
1 teaspoon chopped fresh flat-leaf parsley
Salt and freshly ground black pepper

1. Put the potatoes in a medium saucepan of boiling, salted water, bring back to the boil and simmer for 10 minutes or until just tender. Drain and leave to cool.

2. Melt the butter in a large frying pan over a medium heat. Add the garlic, thyme and rosemary and fry gently for 2 minutes, stirring occasionally.

3. Meanwhile, halve each potato and season with salt and pepper. Place cut-side down in the pan and fry without moving for 10–12 minutes or until golden brown.

4. Preheat the grill to medium. Line the grill pan with foil. Place the potatoes cut-side up on the foil and sprinkle over the Parmesan. Grill for about 5 minutes or until the cheese starts to melt.

5. Transfer the potatoes to a serving platter and sprinkle with parsley. Serve immediately.

SICILIAN-STYLE SAUTÉED POTATOES

Patate saltate in padella alla siciliana

Sicilians claim that the world's best capers are grown in Pantelleria and Salina – both small islands off Sicily. They attribute their superlative qualities to the fertile volcanic soil and climate and always salt the capers rather than preserving them in vinegar or brine. The locals often put them in potato dishes, as they pep up what could otherwise be rather bland. The combination of ingredients in this recipe really capture the punchy, savoury flavours of the Mediterranean.

Serves 4-6

1kg new potatoes (preferably Charlotte), peeled and
  cut into 2cm cubes
3 large garlic cloves, peeled
5 tablespoons olive oil
30g salted butter
6 fresh sage leaves, shredded

16 fresh red cherry tomatoes, halved
100g pitted green olives, drained
100g pitted black olives, drained
20g capers, drained
Salt and freshly ground black pepper

1. Put the potatoes in a medium saucepan of boiling, salted water, bring back to the boil and simmer for 3–4 minutes. Drain and place on kitchen paper to dry.

2. Meanwhile, 'bruise' the garlic by placing the peeled cloves on a board, setting the flat side of a knife on top and pressing down with your palm to flatten slightly.

3. Heat the oil and butter in a large frying pan over a medium heat. Add the garlic, potatoes and sage and season with salt and pepper. Fry for 15 minutes, turning the potatoes every few minutes to ensure even browning (if the garlic starts to burn, remove and discard it).

4. Stir in the tomatoes, both types of olives and capers and fry for 3 minutes. Pile the potatoes on a large serving platter, discard the garlic if you haven't yet done so and serve immediately.

DESSERTS

Sicily

DESSERTS

Mainland Italians would probably get into a heated argument with me about this, but I think that Sicilian desserts might just be Italy's best. Pastries, cakes and cookies were originally made for special occasions or to celebrate a religious feast and all are associated with traditions going back centuries. We visited various patisseries when we were touring Sicily and they really are amazing – their exquisite sweet aromas draw you in from the street and are so irresistible it's simply impossible to walk on by; you have to either stop and admire the window display – or enter and treat yourself.

Probably one of the best known of all Sicilian desserts is cannoli, which are hollow tubes of fried pastry stuffed with a sweet, creamy filling – usually ricotta. They were originally prepared at the beginning of spring and for weddings, their tubular shape apparently symbolising male fertility. Another iconic dessert is cassata siciliana, a wonderful marzipan-encased sponge cake soaked in liqueur and containing ricotta cheese, vanilla and candied fruit. Sicilians also – quite rightly – pride themselves on their ice cream and granitas, which are a kind of upmarket slush puppy.

Chocolate is also a great Sicilian delicacy, particularly in the beautiful Baroque city of Modica, where it is made according to an ancient Aztec recipe and technique brought to Sicily by the Spaniards in the 15th century. Today, it is still made in the traditional way in a process known as 'cold-working', resulting in what many consider the best chocolate in the world – more aromatic and granular than modern chocolate and absolutely divine. Given this legacy, chocolate desserts are plentiful in Sicilian cuisine, but don't worry - you don't have to use chocolate from Modica to make the recipes in this book; all are delicious made with a good-quality chocolate bought from the supermarket.

One final thing: please don't feel daunted by this section. A couple of the recipes might seem a bit elaborate at first glance, but it really is worth making the effort with them as they are so scrumptious and unusual – your pleasure in tasting them and the delight of your family and friends will be your reward!

DESSERTS – SICILY

WATERMELON PUDDINGS

Coppette di anguria

Watermelon pudding is a traditional dessert from Sicily's capital, Palermo. It's usually eaten during the three-day feast of Santa Rosalina in July. It generally includes only three ingredients – watermelon, sugar and cornflour – but the garnishes vary from area to area, ranging from cinnamon, jasmine and pistachios to chocolate chips (which are thought to resemble watermelon seeds). Although it is usually served from one dish for sharing, I think it looks more appealing to serve individual portions.

Serves 6

1.3kg watermelon flesh, cut into chunks
150g caster sugar
100g cornflour
1 teaspoon vanilla extract

200ml double cream
50g dark chocolate chips
20g pistachios, roughly chopped

1. Purée the watermelon flesh in a blender or food processor, or in a bowl using a hand-held blender.

2. Put the sugar and cornflour in a medium saucepan. Tip in the watermelon purée and whisk with a balloon whisk. Transfer the pan to a medium heat and gently bring to the boil, whisking continuously. Reduce the heat to low and continue to whisk for 3 minutes or until the mixture starts to thicken.

3. Remove the pan from the heat and stir in the vanilla. While the mixture is still hot, sieve it into a large heatproof bowl, pressing the fruit through with a spatula or wooden spoon.

4. Divide the mixture evenly between 6 decorative glasses. Leave to cool, cover with cling film and transfer to the fridge for at least 5 hours or overnight.

5. Place the cream in a large bowl and whip until thick enough to hold its shape. To decorate each pudding, spoon a dollop of cream on top and sprinkle over the chocolate chips and pistachios.

JASMINE & ORANGE SORBET

Sorbetto al gelsomino ed arancia

Light and refreshing, sorbet is a fabulous way to end a heavy meal or cleanse your palate between courses. Jasmine and orange make a great combination and bring back memories of walking through groves in summer. Go easy with the jasmine essence, as it can dominate if you're not careful. If you can't find it, add a jasmine tea bag to the cooled mixture and leave it to steep for 1 hour.

Serves 6

100g caster sugar
Sliced zest of 1 unwaxed orange
750ml orange juice from a carton

2 tablespoons freshly squeezed lemon juice
¾ teaspoon jasmine essence

1. Put the sugar in a small saucepan with 250ml water. Heat over a low heat for several minutes until the sugar has dissolved, stirring occasionally. Increase the heat and bring to the boil. Boil for 2 minutes.

2. Add the orange zest, reduce the heat and simmer for 5 minutes. Sieve the mixture into a small bowl (discard the orange zest) and leave to cool completely. Stir in the orange juice and lemon juice and gradually add the jasmine essence, a little at a time and tasting frequently in between additions (you may not want to use it all).

3. Pour the mixture into a 3-litre shallow, freezerproof container, cover and freeze for 4 hours.

4. Remove the sorbet from the freezer and blitz the mixture using a food processor or blender (blitzing will break down the ice crystals). When the sorbet is smooth, thick and slushy, put it back in the freezer for another 2 hours.

5. Remove the sorbet from the freezer and blitz again, as previously. Return to the freezer for a further 2 hours, then repeat the blitzing and freezing process once more.

6. About 10 minutes before serving, remove the sorbet from the freezer to soften slightly. Serve in scoops in small bowls.

PISTACHIO & MARASCHINO CHERRY ICE CREAM

Gelato al pistacchio e ciliege al Maraschino

Known locally as 'green gold', the pistachios grown in Sicily are among the best in the world and the island is the only place in Italy where they are cultivated. Introduced by the Arabs in the 10th century, pistachio trees flourish at the foot of Mount Etna, mainly in Bronte, in eastern Sicily. The island is also known for its superb ice cream, so for this recipe I decided to combine the flavours of vanilla ice cream with pistachios and sweet Maraschino cherries – I must say, it's a real winner.

Serves 6

4 large egg yolks
100g golden caster sugar
1 teaspoon cornflour
300ml double cream

300ml full-fat milk
1 vanilla pod
25g salted pistachios, slightly crushed
60g Maraschino cherries, roughly chopped

1. Put the egg yolks and sugar in a large heatproof bowl and whisk using a balloon whisk until thick, light and fluffy. Add the cornflour and whisk again.

2. Gently warm the double cream and milk in a medium saucepan over a low heat. Split the vanilla pod and, with the back of a knife, scrape the seeds into the cream then drop in the pod. Heat until just below boiling point. Gradually whisk the cream mixture into the egg mixture.

3. Rinse out the saucepan and then pour the mixture back into the pan through a sieve. Discard the vanilla pod. Set the pan over a low heat, stirring constantly until it thickens and you can draw a clear line through the mixture with a wooden spoon (this can take about 10 minutes). Do not boil, or the eggs will curdle.

4. Pour the mixture into a 3-litre shallow, freezerproof container and leave to cool. Cover, transfer to the fridge and chill overnight.

5. Place in the freezer. After 1 hour, remove and whisk the mixture with an electric whisk. Return to the freezer for 1 hour, then whisk again. Freeze once more for a further hour, then whisk in the pistachios and cherries. Return to the freezer for at least 2 hours.

6. Take the container out of the freezer 10 minutes before serving. Scoop the ice cream into bowls.

BAKED PEACHES STUFFED WITH AMARETTI BISCUITS, WALNUTS & RAISINS

Pesche al forno ripiene di amaretti, noci e uva passa

The area around Mount Etna yields peaches that taste as though they must have come from the Garden of Eden. Their flavour intensifies with cooking, and in this dish the amaretti biscuits and walnuts give a crumbly, crunchy texture, the raisins add sweetness and the buttery juices flavoured with amaretto, wine and cinnamon are simply irresistible. Serve hot with vanilla ice cream.

Serves 4

4 ripe peaches, halved and stoned
20g raisins
2 teaspoons amaretto (almond) liqueur
3 amaretti biscuits, crushed
55g golden caster sugar
1 medium egg yolk

1 teaspoon cocoa powder, sieved
20g walnuts, roughly chopped
½ teaspoon ground cinnamon
30g salted butter (room temperature), cut into cubes,
  plus extra for greasing
100ml dry white wine

1. Preheat the oven to 180°C/gas mark 4. Take a peach half and enlarge the stone cavity slightly by removing a little of the flesh with a teaspoon. Chop the removed flesh and set aside. Repeat for all the peaches.

2. Place the raisins in a small bowl or cup, pour over the amaretto liqueur and leave to soak for 20 minutes.

3. To make the filling, put the chopped peach flesh, amaretti biscuits, 40g of the sugar, the egg yolk, cocoa powder, walnuts, cinnamon and half the butter in a small bowl. Mix well. Stir in the raisins and the soaking liquid.

4. Grease a baking dish measuring about 18 x 25cm with butter and place the peaches cut-side up in the dish.

5. Divide the filling between the peach halves, pressing it into each cavity. Sprinkle over the remaining sugar and pour the wine around the fruit. Dot the remaining butter on top of the filling. Bake for 30 minutes. Serve hot.

SESAME BISCUITS

Biscotti di Palermo

Known affectionately as biscotti regina ('queen's biscuits'), these sesame seed delicacies are sold in most bakeries in Palermo and are also available in many other places throughout Sicily. They are soft with a bit of sesame crunch and are delicious served with coffee. Sesame is popular in Sicilian baking, for instance in the well-known bread mafalda, which has a sesame seed crust.

Serves 20

250g plain flour
2 level teaspoons baking powder
½ teaspoon salt
100g salted butter (room temperature)
100g caster sugar

2 large eggs, beaten
1 teaspoon vanilla extract
100ml full-fat milk
100g sesame seeds

1. Preheat the oven to 180°C/gas mark 4. Place the flour, baking powder and salt in a medium bowl. Stir to combine and set aside.

2. Place the butter and sugar in a large bowl and beat together using an electric whisk until light and fluffy. Add half the egg and the vanilla and beat again. Add the remaining egg and 1 tablespoon of the flour mixture and beat again. Add the rest of the flour mixture and stir to form a soft dough. Wrap the dough in cling film and refrigerate for 1 hour.

3. Remove the dough from the fridge, discard the cling film and cut the dough into quarters. Roll each quarter into a sausage shape 25cm long. Cut each length across into 5 pieces.

4. Put the milk in a bowl and the sesame seeds on a plate. Dip each piece of dough first in the milk then roll in the sesame seeds to coat.

5. Line 2 baking sheets with baking parchment. Place the dough pieces on the lined sheets and bake for 25 minutes or until golden. Serve at room temperature.

SICILIAN CASSATA

Cassata siciliana

Sicily's most popular cake, cassata is traditionally from the areas of Palermo and Messina. It is not to be confused with cassata gelata, which is a frozen ice-cream cake. When I was filming for the TV series I visited Corrado Assenza – one of Italy's most renowned pastry chefs – at his Caffé Sicilia in Noto, in the province of Siracusa. He gave me some of his sublime cassata to try and told me all about how the flavours work together to create such a magical concoction. Traditionally, cassata is decorated with glacé fruit, but here I've used fresh fruit dipped in sugar. If you can't find Maraschino liqueur, use kirsch instead.

Serves 10

175g caster sugar
Grated zest and juice of 1 unwaxed lemon
2 tablespoons full-fat milk
1 teaspoon vanilla extract
1 level teaspoon baking powder
6 large eggs, separated
150g plain flour
3 tablespoons Maraschino liqueur

For the marzipan case
400g shop-bought marzipan
1 teaspoon green food colouring
Icing sugar to dust

For the filling
500g ricotta cheese
150g caster sugar

100g mixed peel
100g plain chocolate chips
75g glacé cherries, finely chopped
1 teaspoon vanilla extract
Grated zest and juice of 1 unwaxed orange

For the decoration
50g caster sugar
Variety of soft fruit, e.g. strawberries, cherries, blueberries, redcurrants, figs, etc. (retain any stalks and leaves)

For the glaze
150g icing sugar, sifted
2 tablespoons lemon juice

1. Preheat the oven to 180°C/gas mark 4. Grease a deep, loose-bottomed round cake tin, 20cm diameter, and line with baking parchment.

2. Put the sugar, lemon zest and juice, milk, vanilla and baking powder in a large bowl. Add the egg yolks and beat well using an electric hand whisk for about 2 minutes until pale and creamy.

3. In a separate bowl, whisk the egg whites using a balloon whisk or electric hand whisk on full speed until they form soft peaks. Fold one third of the egg whites into the egg yolk mixture, then carefully tip the yolk mixture into the remaining whites and gently fold trying not to knock out all the air. Fold in the flour, 1 tablespoonful at a time. Tip the mixture into the prepared tin and spread evenly.

4. Bake for 35 minutes or until golden brown, risen and shrinking away from the sides of the tin and a skewer comes out clean when inserted. Leave to cool in the tin for 10 minutes. Run a palette knife around the edge of the tin, turn out the cake, peel off the lining paper and transfer to a wire rack to cool.

5. Use a large, serrated knife to cut the cake horizontally into equal-sized thirds. Drizzle 1 tablespoon of Maraschino liqueur onto each of the cut sides. Line the cake tin with cling film so that it overhangs the sides. Set aside.

6. To make the marzipan case, work the marzipan between your hands so it becomes soft. Gradually add the green colouring, a drop at a time, and work it in thoroughly to ensure even colour distribution. Dust the work surface with icing sugar and roll out the marzipan into a long strip about 10 x 70cm. Cut across into quarters and use the pieces to line the side of the tin (not the bottom), pushing the joins together with your fingers.

7. To make the filling, put the ricotta and sugar in a medium bowl and beat for 2–3 minutes using an electric hand whisk (or wooden spoon) until soft, smooth and well blended. Add the mixed peel, chocolate chips, glacé cherries, vanilla and the zest and juice of the orange and stir well to combine.

8. Place the best-looking piece of cake into the tin (the bottom of your tin will be the top of the cassata, so make sure the golden crust is face down). Spoon over half the ricotta mixture, spread evenly and lay the second layer of cake on top. Repeat with the remaining ricotta and the final piece of cake cut-side down.

9. Bring the cling film up and over the top of the cake so it is completely enclosed and place a couple of food tins on top to weigh down the cakes. Refrigerate for 2 hours.

10. To make the decoration, put the sugar on a plate and roll the fruit in the sugar. If the sugar does not stick well, brush the fruit first with a pastry brush dampened in a little water. Set aside for at least 1 hour or until dry.

11. To invert your cake, hold a large flat serving plate over the top of the tin and turn over both the plate and tin quickly. Ease off the tin and carefully remove the cling film.

12. To make the glaze, put the icing sugar and lemon juice in a bowl and mix to a smooth paste. Gently spread the glaze over the cake using a palette knife so that it covers the top, but try not to let it drip down the sides. Refrigerate for 1 hour until set. Finally, decorate the cake with the frosted fruit.

LEMON & PISTACHIO SPONGE CAKE

Torta al limone e pistacchi

I am dedicating this recipe to two beautiful sisters I met in eastern Sicily – Vera and Saria Calabretta. I spent all day exploring their organic citrus orchard – the Agriturismo San Leonardello – where they grow the most amazing lemons in the region. I have also tried this recipe with fresh oranges and it works just as well. Serve with a little glass of cold limoncello liqueur.

Serves 8

Butter for greasing
Grated zest and juice of 1 large unwaxed lemon
150g caster sugar
80g shelled pistachio nuts, finely chopped

160ml plain full-fat yogurt
150ml sunflower oil
270g self-raising flour
2 large eggs, beaten

1. Preheat the oven to 160°C/gas mark 3. Grease a deep, loose-bottomed round cake tin, 20cm diameter, and line with baking parchment.

2. To make the glaze put the lemon juice in a small bowl, mix in 2 tablespoons of the sugar and set aside.

3. Place the remaining sugar in a large bowl and add the lemon zest, pistachios, yogurt, oil, flour and eggs. Using a wooden spoon, stir to combine for 1 minute.

4. Pour the mixture into the prepared tin and bake for 25–35 minutes or until risen and springy to the touch.

5. Pour the glaze over the cake while it is still hot and leave for 5 minutes to soak in. Remove the cake from the tin and transfer to a wire rack to cool.

FLOURLESS CHOCOLATE CAKE WITH COFFEE CREAM

Torta di cioccolato senza farina e con panna al caffè

This easy chocolate cake has a dense, moist, fudgy texture and an intensely chocolatey flavour. Of course, it is also gluten-free but whether or not you're making it for a coeliac it always goes down a storm, particularly among my chocoholic friends and family. It is sometimes served with orange-flavoured cream, but I prefer the slightly bitter taste of coffee.

Serves 8

225g dark chocolate (about 70% cocoa solids)
100g salted butter
1 teaspoon vanilla extract
4 large eggs, separated
175g icing sugar, sifted, plus extra for dusting
Pinch of salt

For the coffee cream
300ml double cream
1 tablespoon icing sugar, sifted
2 tablespoons strong espresso coffee

1. Preheat the oven to 180°C/gas mark 4. Grease a deep, loose-bottomed round cake tin, 20cm diameter, and line with baking parchment.

2. Break the chocolate into a large heatproof bowl, add the butter and vanilla and set the bowl over a pan of gently simmering water. The base of the bowl should not touch the water. Leave until just melted, then remove the pan from the heat, stir, and leave the chocolate to cool slightly. Alternatively, melt the mixture in the microwave on high in short bursts, stirring in between.

3. Put the egg yolks, icing sugar and salt in another large bowl and whisk using an electric whisk for about 2 minutes or until thick and creamy.

4. Place the egg whites in a medium bowl and whisk with an electric hand whisk on full speed until they form stiff peaks.

5. Fold the melted chocolate into the egg-yolk mixture, then gently fold in the whites in 3 batches. Use a metal spoon to fold in the whites in a figure-of-eight motion, cutting through the mixture and turning it over until well blended.

6. Pour the mixture into the prepared tin and spread evenly. Bake for 25 minutes or until risen and shrinking away from the sides of the tins. Leave to cool in the tin before turning out onto a serving plate. Dust with icing sugar.

7. To make the coffee cream, put the cream in a bowl and whip using a balloon whisk or an electric hand whisk on low speed until it forms soft peaks. Fold in the icing sugar and coffee. Serve alongside the cake.

MELTING CHOCOLATE FONDANTS WITH TRUFFLES AND MARSALA

Coppette di cioccolato con tartufi al cacao e Marsala

When I was filming in Modica I visited Antica Dolceria – the oldest chocolate establishment in town. Pierpaolo Ruta, the owner of the shop, told me all about the magical world of chocolate and together we came up with the idea of these melting chocolate fondants. Always use good-quality chocolate, and if you prefer you can substitute the Marsala with sherry or orange liqueur. If you don't have dariole moulds, use ramekins instead. Serve with a little glass of Marsala.

Serves 6

200g plain dark chocolate, 70% cocoa solids
100g salted butter (room temperature)
2 large eggs, separated
40g cornflour
40g ground almonds

90g caster sugar
2 tablespoons Marsala wine
6 chocolate truffles
Icing sugar, sifted, for dusting

1. Preheat the oven to 180°C/gas mark 4. Finely grate 60g of the chocolate onto a plate. Grease the insides of 6 tall dariole moulds (measuring about 5 x 8cm) with half the butter and dust with the grated chocolate (shake off any excess and reserve). Place the moulds on a baking sheet and set aside.

2. Place the remaining butter and chocolate (plus any unused grated chocolate) in a large heatproof bowl and set the bowl over a pan of gently simmering water. The base of the bowl should not touch the water. Leave until just melted, then remove the pan from the heat.

3. Stir in the egg yolks, cornflour and almonds. Leave to cool slightly.

4. Place the egg whites in a medium bowl and whisk with an electric hand whisk on full speed until they form stiff peaks. Gradually stir in the caster sugar 1 tablespoon at a time, continuing to whisk, until the whites are glossy. Fold the egg-white mixture and Marsala into the cooled (but not set) melted chocolate in 2 batches.

5. Carefully spoon half the mixture into the moulds, place a truffle on top then continue to fill the moulds, leaving a 5mm gap at the top.

6. Bake the fondants for 12–14 minutes or until risen and still slightly wobbly. Carefully turn them out onto 6 plates and dust lightly with icing sugar. Serve immediately.

SWEET PASTRY SHELLS FILLED WITH RICOTTA & CHOCOLATE CHIPS

Cannoli ripieni di ricotta e gocce di cioccolato

Probably the most classic of all Sicilian desserts, cannoli are tube-shaped shells of fried pastry dough filled with a sweet, creamy filling, usually sheep's milk ricotta. Traditionally, a piece of cane was used to wrap the dough around, as cane doesn't burn in hot oil. Today, you can buy metal cannoli tubes from kitchen shops or online.

Makes 20

300g plain flour, plus extra for dusting

75g caster sugar

1 pinch of salt

50g salted butter (room temperature)

130ml dry white wine

About 1 litre vegetable oil for deep-frying

For the filling

800g ricotta cheese

400g icing sugar, sifted

Grated zest of 1 unwaxed orange

200g dark chocolate chips

For the decoration

Icing sugar for dusting

Pistachios, finely chopped (optional)

1. Put the flour, sugar and salt in a large bowl. Add the butter and rub it in, then pour in the wine. Mix together using your hands until thoroughly combined and able to hold together in a ball. Knead the dough on a lightly floured surface for about 5 minutes. Wrap in cling film and chill overnight.

2. Unwrap the dough and knead for a further 5 minutes. Lightly dust a rolling pin with flour and dust the dough and the worksurface. Roll out the dough to form a rectangle about 3mm thick. Cut out 5 circles using a 10cm plain biscuit cutter. Place a cannoli tube on top of each dough circle and roll the dough around the tube. Use a little cold water to seal the edges.

3. Heat a deep-fat fryer to 190°C, or heat the oil in a deep pan or a wok. To test the temperature, add a tiny piece of bread; it will sizzle when the oil is hot enough for frying.

4. Lower the pastry tubes into the hot oil, 5 at a time, and fry for 2 minutes or until golden brown, turning halfway through cooking. Remove and drain on kitchen paper.

5. Once cool enough to handle, carefully twist the cannoli tubes to release the pastry shells. Set the shells aside to cool on a wire rack. Wipe the tubes and use them for making the remaining shells.

6. Meanwhile, to make the filling, put the ricotta, icing sugar and orange zest in a bowl. Beat using a hand-held electric whisk or wooden spoon until smooth. Fold in the chocolate chips and chill for 2 hours.

7. Just before serving, fill the pastry shells with the ricotta mixture using a piping bag. Fill from the centre to one end, then repeat on the other side. Dust with icing sugar and dip the ends in the pistachios (if using).

INDEX

First published in Great Britain in 2015
by Hodder & Stoughton
An Hachette UK company

1

Copyright © ITV Ventures Ltd 2015

Recipes copyright © Gino D'Acampo Ltd 2015

Television series Gino's Italian Escape: Islands in the Sun
Copyright © ITV Studios Limited 2015. Licensed by ITV
Ventures Ltd. All rights reserved.

Photography copyright © Matt Russell 2015, except page 133
(top) from author's collection.

A CIP catalogue record for this title is available from the British
Library

Hardback ISBN 978 1 473 61964 7
Ebook ISBN 978 1 473 61965 4

Editorial Director: Nicky Ross
Editor: Sarah Hammond
Project Editor: Polly Boyd
Designer: Georgia Vaux
Photographer: Matt Russell
Food Stylist: Gee Charman
Props Stylist: Rebecca Newport

Typeset in Whitney

Printed and bound in Germany by Mohn

Hodder & Stoughton policy is to use papers that are natural,
renewable and recyclable products and made from wood grown
in sustainable forests. The logging and manufacturing processes
are expected to conform to the environmental regulations of the
country of origin.

Hodder & Stoughton Ltd
Carmelite House
50 Victoria Embankment
London EC4Y 0DZ

www.hodder.co.uk

A note from the author

When I was in Sardinia I met a local
poet called Salvatore Ruzittu, who
is famous in the Gallura region for
writing poems about the island and its
food. I asked him to write a poem for
this book, and here it is:

Benvinuti in Gaddhura

Amichi turisti, viniti in Gaddhura!
Eu v'aspettu assai ulinteri
A magna' mazzafissa cu lu meli,
O puru cjusoni fatti a scaatura
È li puliggjoni di broccju o di cascju.
Bonapittittu a tutti cu un bascju!

Welcome to Gallura

Welcome tourist friends, who have come to Gallura!
You are welcomed with open arms
To eat our ricotta with honey,
Our freshly made gnocchetti sardi
And home-made ravioli filled with cheese.
Buon appetito to you all, and a kiss!